The Institute of Chartered Accountants in England and Wales

# ACCOUNTING

Professional Stage Knowledge Level

For exams in 2012

**Question Bank**

www.icaew.com

Accounting
The Institute of Chartered Accountants in England and Wales Professional Stage

ISBN: 978-0-85760-217-6
First edition 2007
Fifth edition 2011

British Library Cataloguing-in-Publication Data
A catalogue record for this book has been applied for from the British Library

Printed in Great Britain

Your learning materials are printed on paper sourced from sustainable,
managed forests.

# Contents

# Question Bank

Your exam will consist of 40 questions worth 2.5 marks each, together adding up to 100 marks. You should complete them all.

The questions are of two types:

- **Multiple choice** – select 1 from 4 options A, B, C or D (see Chapter 6 Q1)

- **Multiple response** – select 2 or 3 responses from 4 to 10 options (see Chapter 6 Q10)

**In your exam you will not have to complete any linked multiple choice questions which share the same data, nor will any questions require numerical entry.**

In this Question Bank you should select only one option per question unless told otherwise.

1   Which of the following best explains what is meant by 'capital expenditure'?

Capital expenditure is expenditure:

A   On non-current assets, including repairs and maintenance

B   On expensive items over £10,000

C   On the acquisition of non-current assets, or improvement in their earning capacity

D   On items relating to owners' capital

LO 1c

2   Which of the following should be accounted for as capital expenditure?

A   The annual cost of painting a factory floor

B   The repair of a window in a building

C   The purchase of a vehicle by a garage for re-sale

D   Legal fees incurred on the purchase of a building

LO 1c

3   Which of the following items should be treated as capital expenditure in the financial statements of a sole trader?

A   £500 taken by the proprietor to buy himself a hi-fi system

B   £400 spent on purchasing a new PC to replace his secretary's old one

C   £2,000 on purchasing a machine for resale

D   £150 paid to a painter for redecorating his office

LO 1c

4   Which of the following is an aspect of relevance, according to the *Conceptual Framework for Financial Reporting*?

A   Neutrality

B   Free from error

C   Completeness

D   Materiality

LO 1a

5    According to the *Conceptual Framework for Financial Reporting,* which qualitative characteristics enhance the usefulness of information that is relevant and faithfully represented?

A    Comparability, understandability, timeliness, verifiability

B    Consistency, prudence, measurability, verifiability

C    Consistency, reliability, measurability, timeliness

D    Materiality, understandability, measurability, reliability

LO 1a

6    Which THREE of the following users of financial statements are likely to be interested in the financial statements of a small private company?

A    Stock market analysts

B    Company employees

C    The company's bank

D    Institutional shareholders

E    Suppliers

LO 1a

7    Which TWO of the following information needs apply to the government and its agencies in relation to the business of a sole trader?

The government and its agencies need information to

A    Establish levels of tax revenue

B    Assess whether the business will continue in existence

C    Produce national statistics

D    Assess the owner's stewardship

E    Take decisions about their investment

LO 1a

8    Information about an entity's financial position is primarily provided in

A    The income statement

B    The statement of financial position

C    Retained earnings

D    The statement of cash flows

LO 1a

9 According to the *Conceptual Framework for Financial Reporting,* information on which TWO of the following areas can help users identify the reporting entity's financial strengths and weaknesses?

A The economic resources it controls

B Its financial performance in the past

C The demographic structure of the local economy

D The entity's claims (the entity's liabilities)

E Its management structure

LO 1a

10 According to IAS 1 (revised) *Presentation of Financial Statements* which TWO of the following are objectives of financial statements?

A To show the results of management's stewardship of the resources entrusted to it

B To provide a basis for valuing the entity

C To provide information about the financial position, financial performance and cash flows of an entity that is useful to a wide range of users in making economic decisions

D To facilitate comparison of financial performance between entities operating in different industries

E To assist management and those charged with governance in making timely economic decisions about deployment of the entity's resources

LO 1a

11 Information is relevant if it is capable of making a difference in the decisions made by users. According to the *Conceptual Framework for Financial Reporting* financial information is capable of making a difference in decisions if it has which of the following?

1 Predictive value

2 Comparative value

3 Historic value

4 Confirmatory value

A 1 and 3 only

B 2 and 4 only

C 1 and 4 only

D 2 and 3 only

LO 1c

12 The accounting principle which, in times of rising prices, tends to understate asset values and overstate profits, is

A Going concern

B Accruals

C Consistency

D Historical cost

13    In times of rising prices, what effect does the use of the historical cost concept have on a company's asset values and profit?

    A    Asset values and profit both understated

    B    Asset values and profit both overstated

    C    Asset values understated and profit overstated

    D    Asset values overstated and profit understated

14    Which of the following statements about accounting concepts and the characteristics of financial information is correct?

    A    The concept of substance over form means that the legal interpretation of a transaction must be reflected in financial statements, regardless of the economic substance.

    B    The historical cost concept means that only items capable of being measured in monetary terms can be recognised in financial statements.

    C    It may sometimes be necessary to exclude information that is relevant and reliable from financial statements because it is too difficult for some users to understand.

    D    A specific disclosure requirement of an IAS need not be satisfied if the information is immaterial

15    Listed below are some comments on accounting conventions.

    1    According to the *Conceptual Framework for Financial Reporting*, financial information must be either relevant or faithfully represented if it is to be useful.

    2    Materiality means that only items having a physical existence may be recognised as assets.

    3    The substance over form convention means that the legal interpretation of a transaction must always be shown in financial statements, even if this differs from the commercial effect.

    Which, if any, of these comments is correct?

    A    1 only

    B    2 only

    C    3 only

    D    None of them

16 Which of the following is the best description of fair presentation in accordance with IAS 1 (revised) *Presentation of Financial Statements*?

    A    The financial statements are accurate

    B    The financial statements are as accurate as possible given the accounting systems of the organisation

    C    The directors of the company have stated that the financial statements are accurate and correctly prepared

    D    The financial statements are reliable in that they reflect the effects of transactions, other events and conditions

LO 1c

17 Which of the following definitions for the 'going concern' concept in accounting is the most accurate in the light of IAS 1 (revised) *Presentation of Financial Statements*?

    A    'The directors do not intend to liquidate the entity or to cease trading in the foreseeable future'

    B    'The entity is able to pay its debts as and when they fall due'

    C    'The directors expect the entity's assets to yield future economic benefits'

    D    'Financial statements have been prepared on the assumption that the entity is solvent and would be able to pay all creditors in full in the event of being wound up'

LO 3b

18 According to IAS 1 (revised) *Presentation of Financial Statements*, compliance with International Accounting Standards and International Financial Reporting Standards will normally ensure that

    A    The entity's inventory is valued at net realisable value

    B    The entity's assets are valued at their break-up value

    C    The entity's financial statements are prepared on the assumption that it is a going concern

    D    The entity's financial position, financial performance and cash flows are presented fairly

LO 1c, 3b

19 The directors of Lagon plc wish to omit an item from the company's financial statements on the grounds that it is commercially sensitive. Information on the item would influence the users of the information when making economic decisions. According to IAS 1 (revised) *Presentation of Financial Statements* the item is said to be

    A    Neutral

    B    Prudent

    C    Material

    D    Understandable

LO 1a

# Chapter 2: The accounting equation

1     The accounting equation can be written as:

    A     Assets + profits – drawings – liabilities = closing capital

    B     Assets – liabilities – drawings = opening capital + profit

    C     Assets – liabilities – opening capital + drawings = profit

    D     Opening capital + profit – drawings – liabilities = assets

LO 1c

2     The capital of a sole trader would change as a result of

    A     A credit customer paying by cheque

    B     Raw materials being purchased on credit

    C     Non-current assets being purchased on credit

    D     Personal petrol being paid for out of the business's petty cash

LO 1c, 3a

3     A business can make a profit and yet have a decreased bank balance. Which of the following might cause this to happen?

    A     The sale of non-current assets at a loss

    B     The charging of depreciation in the income statement

    C     The lengthening of the period of credit given to customers

    D     The lengthening of the period of credit taken from suppliers

LO 1c, 3a, 3b

4     The purpose of the financial statement that lists an entity's total assets and total capital/liabilities is to show

    A     The financial performance of the entity over a period of time

    B     The amount the entity could be sold for in liquidation

    C     The amount the entity could be sold for as a going concern

    D     The financial position of the entity at a particular moment in time

LO 3b, 3a

5    A sole trader is £5,000 overdrawn at her bank and receives £1,000 from a credit customer in respect of its account.

Which elements of the accounting equation will change due to this transaction?

A    Assets and liabilities only

B    Liabilities only

C    Assets only

D    Assets, liabilities and capital

LO 1c

6    A sole trader purchases goods on credit.

Which elements of the accounting equation will change due to this transaction?

A    Assets and liabilities

B    Assets and capital

C    Capital and liabilities

D    Assets only

LO 1c

7    A sole trader borrows £10,000 from a bank.

Which elements of the accounting equation will change due to this transaction?

A    Assets and liabilities

B    Assets and capital

C    Capital and liabilities

D    Assets only

LO 1c

8    A sole trader sells goods for cash for £500 which had cost £300.

Which elements of the accounting equation will change due to this transaction?

A    Assets and liabilities

B    Assets and capital

C    Capital and liabilities

D    Assets only

LO 1c

9   A sole trader increases the business's number of motor vehicles by adding his own car to its fleet.

Which elements of the accounting equation will change due to this transaction?

A   Assets only

B   Capital only

C   Assets and capital

D   Assets and liabilities

LO 1c

10  Which THREE of the following are elements of financial statements as identified by the *Conceptual Framework for Financial Reporting*?

A   Income

B   Expenses

C   Profits

D   Losses

E   Obligations

F   Resources

G   Equity

LO 1c

1   A business paid out £12,450 in net wages to its employees. In respect of these wages, the following amounts were shown in the statement of financial position.

|                              |               | £     |
|------------------------------|---------------|-------|
| PAYE payable                 |               | 2,480 |
| National Insurance payable   | – employees'  | 1,350 |
|                              | – employer's  | 1,500 |

No other deductions were made.

Employees' gross wages, before deductions, were

A   £12,450

B   £27,450

C   £16,280

D   £17,780

LO 1c

---

2   Books of original entry in a standard double entry bookkeeping system are used to list similar transactions with the totals being posted to the nominal ledger.

A   True

B   False

The sales day book is the book of original entry for discount allowed to customers.

C   True

D   False

LO 1b, 1c

---

3   Which of the following best explains the imprest system of petty cash?

A   Each month an equal amount of cash is transferred into petty cash

B   The exact amount of petty cash expenditure is reimbursed at intervals to maintain a fixed float

C   Petty cash must be kept under lock and key

D   The petty cash total must never fall below the imprest amount

LO 1b, 1c

---

4    Which of the following is a book of original entry?

    A    Nominal ledger

    B    Journal

    C    Receivables ledger

    D    Asset register

LO 1b, 1c

5    The following data has been extracted from the payroll records of Kleen Ltd for the month of February 20X1.

|                        | £      |
|------------------------|-------:|
| PAYE                   | 17,000 |
| Employer's NIC         | 7,500  |
| Employees' NIC         | 6,000  |
| Cash paid to employees | 50,000 |

The wage expense for the month is

    A    £50,000

    B    £56,000

    C    £74,500

    D    £80,500

LO 1b, 1c

6    When a purchase invoice is received from a supplier which TWO of the following documents would the invoice be checked to?

    A    Sales order

    B    Purchase order

    C    Remittance advice

    D    Goods received note

    E    Credit note

LO 1b

7    G purchases goods on credit from H for £1,000. £100 of these goods are defective and G returns them to H. What document would H issue to G in respect of the returned goods?

    A    Invoice

    B    Remittance advice

    C    Credit note

    D    Delivery note

LO 1b

8    In which book of original entry would discounts allowed be recorded?

    A    Sales day book

    B    Purchases day book

    C    Cash book

    D    Journal

LO 1b

---

9    In which book of original entry is VAT on credit sales recorded?

    A    Sales day book

    B    Purchases day book

    C    Cash book

    D    Journal

LO 1b

---

10   In which book of original entry is VAT on purchases from non-credit suppliers recorded?

    A    Sales day book

    B    Purchases day book

    C    Cash book

    D    Journal

LO 1b

---

11   The petty cash float in a business has an imprest amount of £200. At the end of March vouchers in the petty cash box totalled £136 and the amount of cash remaining in the box was £54.

    Which of the following explains the difference?

    A    A petty cash voucher for £10 is missing

    B    An employee was given £10 too little when making a petty cash claim

    C    An employee reimbursed petty cash with £10 in respect of postage stamps used, but no voucher was prepared

    D    A voucher for £10 was put in the box but no payment was made to the employee

LO 1b

---

12    A business has the following payroll costs for a month:

|  |  | £ |
| --- | --- | --- |
| Gross pay |  | 38,600 |
| Income tax |  | 5,400 |
| Employee's national insurance |  | 3,100 |
| Employer's national insurance |  | 3,500 |

What is the wages cost to the business for the month?

A    £38,600

B    £42,100

C    £47,100

D    £50,600

LO 1b, 1c

13    Which TWO of the following are source documents that are recorded in an entity's books of original entry?

A    Goods received note

B    Invoice to a customer

C    Purchase order to a supplier

D    Cheque to a supplier

E    Delivery note to a customer

LO 1b

14    Johan plc enters into the following transactions in relation to Marius plc, a supplier which is also a customer.  Which of Johan plc's accounting records is affected by each of these transactions?

Marius plc buys goods from Johan plc on credit terms

A    Sales day book

B    Purchase day book

C    Payables ledger

Johan plc agrees to make contra entries in Marius plc's personal accounts in its accounting system.

D    Sales day book

E    Purchase day book

F    Payables ledger

LO 1b

1   Richard is a VAT registered trader whose sales and purchases carry VAT at the standard rate of 20%. Richard sells a customer goods on credit for £4,800 exclusive of VAT. The double entry to record this transaction is

    A    Debit Sales £4,800, Debit VAT £960, Credit Receivables £5,760

    B    Debit Sales £4,000, Debit VAT £800, Credit Receivables £4,800

    C    Debit Receivables £5,760, Credit Sales £4,800, Credit VAT £960

    D    Debit Receivables £4,800, Credit Sales £4,000, Credit VAT £800

LO 1c, 2d

2   What transaction is represented by the entries: debit rent, credit landlord?

    A    The receipt of rental income by the business

    B    The issue of an invoice for rent to a tenant

    C    The receipt of an invoice for rent payable by the business

    D    The payment of rent by the business

LO 1c, 2d

3   In double-entry bookkeeping, which of the following statements is true?

    A    Credit entries decrease liabilities and increase income

    B    Debit entries decrease income and increase assets

    C    Credit entries decrease expenses and increase assets

    D    Debit entries decrease expenses and increase assets

LO 1c

4   The VAT account in Atomic Ltd's nominal ledger currently shows output tax and input tax for the quarter at £228,816 and £176,949 respectively. A detailed review of the account highlights the following matters:

    1    £8,301 of VAT on invoices received has been posted to output tax

    2    VAT of £3,606 on sales has been posted to the debit of the VAT account

The correct amount payable to HM Revenue and Customs is

    A    £47,172

    B    £35,265

    C    £59,079

    D    £42,477

LO 1c

5    A debit balance of £3,000 brought down on A Ltd's account in B Ltd's books means that

B Ltd owes A Ltd £3,000.

A    True

B    False

LO 1c

6    The double entry to record a settlement or cash discount granted by a supplier is

A    Debit Payables, Credit Discounts allowed

B    Debit Payables, Credit Discounts received

C    Debit Discounts received, Credit Payables

D    Debit Discounts allowed, Credit Payables

LO 1c

7    Winn Ltd has opening trade payables of £24,183 and closing trade payables of £34,655. Purchases for the period totalled £254,192 (£31,590 relating to cash purchases).

Total payments recorded in the payables ledger for the period were

A    £212,130

B    £233,074

C    £243,720

D    £264,664

LO 1c, 2d

8    In relation to books of original entry and double entry bookkeeping for an entity which is registered for VAT, which one of the following statements is correct?

A    The payables ledger column in the cash payments book is debited to the purchases account in the nominal ledger

B    Purchases and VAT in the purchases day book are recorded in the nominal ledger as debit entries to the purchases and VAT accounts and as a credit entry in the payables control account

C    The cash receipt recorded in the petty cash book when the petty cash is topped up is recorded as a debit entry in the main cash book

D    VAT recorded in the cash book in respect of purchases is credited to the VAT account

LO 1c, 2d

9    What is the correct double entry for the posting of the discounts received column in the cash payments book?

A    Debit Discounts received, Credit Receivables

B    Debit Payables, Credit Discounts received

C    Debit Receivables, Credit Discounts received

D    Debit Discounts received, Credit Payables

LO 1c, 2d

10   Which of the following could be a debit entry in the payables account?

A    Purchases day book total

B    Cash purchases total

C    Payables ledger total in the cash book

D    Discounts allowed total from cash book

LO 1c, 2d

11   What is the correct treatment of a trade discount received from a credit supplier?

A    Recorded in the purchases day book

B    Deducted from the list price with the net amount recorded in the purchases day book

C    Recorded in the journal

D    Deducted from the invoice total with the net amount recorded in the cash book

LO 1b, 1c, 2d

12   What is the correct double entry for discounts allowed?

A    Debit Discounts allowed, Credit Receivables

B    Debit Discounts allowed, Credit Payables

C    Debit Receivables, Credit Discounts allowed

D    Debit Payables, Credit Discounts allowed

LO 1c, 2d

13  A business which is registered for VAT received the following invoice from one of its VAT registered suppliers:

| Invoice: | 7035 | |
| --- | --- | --- |
| Date: | 20 December 20X0 | |
| | | £ |
| | Goods: 100 @ £10 | 1,000 |
| | Less:   Trade discount | (50) |
| | | 950 |

A further discount of £50 will be allowed if payment is received within 14 days.

What amount of VAT should have been charged on the invoice?

A    £180

B    £190

C    £200

D    £210

1   The following are all current assets; trade receivables, inventories, prepaid expenses and cash at bank. Which is the least liquid?

   A   Trade receivables

   B   Inventories

   C   Prepaid expenses

   D   Cash at bank

LO 3c

2   Which of the following would be classified as a non-current asset?

   A   Cash

   B   Prepayments

   C   Land

   D   Receivables

LO 3c

3   When preparing an extended trial balance what are the entries for the business's profit?

   A   Debit the statement of financial position column and the income statement column

   B   Credit the statement of financial position column and the income statement column

   C   Debit the statement of financial position column and credit the income statement column

   D   Debit the income statement column and credit the statement of financial position column

LO 2c

4   Which of the following statements concerning preparation of financial statements is true?

   A   The balances on income and expense accounts are brought down at the end of the accounting period to be carried forward to the next accounting period

   B   The balances on asset and liability accounts are summarised in an additional ledger account known as the statement of financial position ledger account

   C   The profit and loss ledger account is a list of all the balances extracted from the business's accounts

   D   A net loss is a credit entry in the profit and loss ledger account

LO 3c

5    A sole trader had receivables of £2,700 at 1 May and during May made cash sales of £7,200, credit sales of £16,500 and received £15,300 from his customers.

The balance on his receivables account at the end of May was

A    £1,500

B    £3,900

C    £8,700

D    £11,100

LO 3c

6    Which TWO of the following types of account would normally appear on the debit side of the trial balance?

A    Asset

B    Liability

C    Income

D    Expense

E    Capital

LO 1e

7    Which of the following would be a credit balance in the trial balance?

A    Bank overdraft

B    Drawings

C    Discounts allowed

D    Carriage outwards

LO 1e

8    Which of the following statements concerning the extended trial balance is correct?

A    If the initial trial balance balances an error may still have been made

B    The closing inventories balance is included in the initial trial balance

C    The owner's drawings taken in the period are shown in the adjustments columns of the extended trial balance

D    Non-current assets appear in the credit column of the statement of financial position

LO 2c

9   Plym plc is a retailer which is registered for VAT. All sales, and all purchases of goods for resale, attract VAT at the rate of 20%. For the year to 30 June 20X7 Plym plc paid £69,600 to suppliers in respect of goods for resale, and showed revenue in the income statement of £89,400. There was no change in the figures for inventory and trade payables in the statements of financial position as at 30 June 20X6 and 20X7.

What was Plym plc's gross profit for the year ended 30 June 20X7?

A   £19,800

B   £4,900

C   £31,400

D   £16,500

LO 1c

1   In a business that uses control accounts, which of the following errors could result in a suspense account being required to balance the trial balance?

  A   Cash received from receivables treated as a cash sale

  B   A supplier's invoice for £32 recorded as £23 in the purchases account

  C   Payments to suppliers of £647 recorded as £674 in the payables ledger

  D   One page lost from the purchase day book

LO 2b

2   Anthony's business bank statement showed an overdrawn balance of £5,250 on 31 October 20X1. When this was reconciled to the cash book, the following differences were noted:

|  | £ |
|---|---|
| Unpresented cheques | 1,070 |
| Uncredited lodgements | 1,240 |
| Standing order for insurance premium payable not entered in the cash book | 890 |
| Overdraft interest not recorded in the cash book | 80 |
| Credited in error to Anthony's account by the bank | 300 |

What was the original balance on Anthony's cash book at 31 October 20X1?

  A   £4,450 credit

  B   £4,410 credit

  C   £2,940 credit

  D   £1,670 debit

LO 2b

3   The following receivables control account contains a number of errors:

RECEIVABLES CONTROL ACCOUNT

| 20X5 | | £ | 20X5 | | £ |
|---|---|---|---|---|---|
| 1.1 | Balance b/d | 414,000 | 31.1 | Credit sales | 101,000 |
| 31.1 | Cash from credit customers | 111,000 | 31.1 | Discounts allowed | 1,400 |
| 31.1 | Contra against suppliers | 6,650 | 31.1 | Irrecoverable debts written off | 13,600 |
| | | | 31.1 | Balance c/d | 415,650 |
| | | 531,650 | | | 531,650 |

What should the closing balance be once the errors are corrected?

  A   £382,350

  B   £385,150

  C   £395,650

  D   £409,550

LO 2b

4    As at 31 December 20X1 a company's bank statement shows an overdraft of £1,500. The statement includes bank charges of £30 which have not yet been recorded in the company's cash book. On 29 December 20X1 the company had paid a cheque of £500 to a supplier and banked £200 received from a trade receivable; neither of these items appear in the bank statement.

The overdraft on the company's statement of financial position at 31 December 20X1 should be

A    £1,800

B    £1,830

C    £1,200

D    £1,230

LO 2b

5    A company's trial balance failed to agree, the totals being:

Debit       £815,602

Credit     £808,420

Which of the following errors could fully account for the difference?

A    The omission from the trial balance of the prepayments asset account £7,182

B    Discounts allowed of £3,591 debited to the discounts received account, in error

C    No entries made in the records for cash purchases totalling £7,182

D    Bank overdraft of £3,591 was included in the trial balance as a debit

LO 1e

6    If the trial balance does not balance an error must have been made.

A    True

B    False

Closing inventory balance is always included in the initial trial balance.

C    True

D    False

LO 1e

7    The owner's drawings are shown on the trial balance.

A    True

B    False

The closing inventory balance is included in the extended trial balance.

C    True

D    False

LO 1e

8   If a supplier's credit note of £130 has been entered as an invoice in the purchases day book, but has been correctly entered in the supplier's payables ledger account, the totals of the debit column and the credit column on the subsequently extracted trial balance would

A   Agree

B   Show £260 more on the debit than the credit side

C   Show £260 more on the credit than the debit side

D   Be different by £130

LO 1e

9   Clanger plc has a reporting period for the year ended 31 December 20X1. At that date the balance on the receivables control account was £65,000, but the total of the individual accounts in the receivables ledger came to £63,620.

Upon investigation the following facts were discovered:

1   The sales day book total for week 49 had been overcast by £300.

2   A credit balance of £210 on Cabbage's account in the receivables ledger had been incorrectly treated as a debit entry, when balancing off his account.

3   A payables ledger contra of £1,500 has been entered in Sprout's account in the receivables ledger but no other entry had been made.

The correct balance on both the receivables ledger listing and the receivables control account is

A   £62,900

B   £63,200

C   £63,400

D   £66,800

LO 3c

10   When performing a reconciliation between the bank statement and the cash book, which TWO of the following would require an entry in the cash book?

A   Deposits credited after date

B   Direct debit on bank statement only

C   Bank charges

D   Bank error

E   Cheque presented after date

LO 2b

11  On 1 December 20X0 Gilbert's payables control account had a balance of £3,200. During the month the following transactions occurred:

Payments to suppliers  £2,500
Cash purchases  £800
Purchases on credit  £3,300
Returns outwards of credit purchases  £750

The control account balance as at 31 December 20X0 is

A    £3,250

B    £3,300

C    £3,550

D    £4,000

LO 2b

12  Which of the following errors would result in a trial balance imbalance?

A    The discounts allowed balance was listed as a credit on the trial balance

B    Drawings for the last month of the year had been posted to the sundry expenses account

C    A contra settlement had been recorded only in the sales and purchases ledgers

D    Capital expenditure had been posted to repairs

LO 1e

13  The credit side of a trial balance totals £400 more than the debit side. Which of the following errors would fully account for the difference?

A    £200 paid for lawnmower repairs has been correctly entered in the cash book and credited to the lawnmower asset account.

B    Discount received £200 has been debited to the discount allowed account.

C    A receipt of £400 for commission receivable has been omitted from the records.

D    The petty cash balance of £200 has been omitted from the trial balance.

LO 1e

14  The following bank reconciliation has been partially completed:

|  | £ |
|---|---|
| Balance per bank statement (overdrawn) | 73,680 |
| Uncredited lodgements | 102,480 |
| Unpresented cheques | 87,240 |

What should the cash book balance be?

A    £88,920 credit

B    £88,920 debit

C    £58,440 debit

D    £58,440 credit

LO 2b

15  Which of the following errors would still result in a balanced trial balance?

A    The opening inventory balance was omitted from the nominal ledger.

B    A transposition error was made when posting cash received from a credit customer to the receivables ledger.

C    The discounts received balance was listed as a debit on the trial balance.

D    The total column of the cash payments book was miscast.

LO 1e

16  The following payables control account for an entity where all goods are purchased on credit contains some errors.

PAYABLES CONTROL ACCOUNT

| | £ | | £ |
|---|---|---|---|
| Purchases | 481,600 | Opening balance | 192,300 |
| Discounts received | 6,300 | Cash paid to suppliers | 494,200 |
| Contras with receivables | 2,100 | Cash refunds | 8,700 |
| Closing balance | 205,200 | | |
| | 695,200 | | 695,200 |

What will the closing balance be when the errors have been corrected?

A    £180,000

B    £184,200

C    £162,600

D    £192,600

LO 2b

17  Which of the following errors would cause a trial balance imbalance?

   A   The discounts received column of the cash book was overcast

   B   Cash paid for the purchase of office furniture was debited to the general expenses account

   C   The discounts allowed column of the cash book was undercast

   D   A cheque paid for general expenses was correct in the cash book and was credited to non-current assets

LO 1e

18  Your cash book at 31 December 20X3 shows a bank balance of £565 overdrawn. On comparing this with your bank statement at the same date, you discover the following.

   1   A cheque for £57 drawn by you on 29 December 20X3 has not yet been presented for payment.

   2   A cheque for £92 from a customer, which was paid into the bank on 24 December 20X3, has been dishonoured on 31 December 20X3.

   The correct balance in your cash book as at 31 December 20X3 is

   A   £473 DR

   B   £714 CR

   C   £657 CR

   D   £473 CR

LO 2b

19  The debit side of a trial balance totals £800 more than the credit side.

   Which of the following errors would fully account for the difference?

   A   £400 paid for plant maintenance has been correctly entered in the cash book and credited to the plant asset account.

   B   Discount received of £400 has been debited to discount allowed account.

   C   A receipt of £800 for rent receivable has been omitted from the records.

   D   The petty cash balance of £800 has been omitted from the trial balance.

LO 1e

20  Where a transaction is entered into the correct ledger accounts, but the wrong amount is used, the error is known as an error of

   A   Omission

   B   Original entry

   C   Commission

   D   Principle

LO 2a

21  The following information relates to a bank reconciliation. The balance in the cash book before taking the items below into account was £8,970 overdrawn.

(i)   Bank charges of £550 on the bank statement have not been entered in the cash book.

(ii)  The bank has credited the account in error with £425 which belongs to another customer.

(iii) Cheque payments totalling £3,275 have been entered in the cash book but have not been presented for payment.

(iv) Cheques totalling £5,380 have been correctly entered on the debit side of the cash book but have not been paid in at the bank.

What was the overdrawn balance as shown by the bank statement?

A    £6,990

B    £10,650

C    £11,200

D    £11,625

LO 2b

22  The cash book shows a bank balance of £5,675 overdrawn at 31 August 20X5. It is subsequently discovered that a standing order payment for £125 has been entered twice, and that a dishonoured cheque for £450 has been debited in the cash book instead of credited.

The correct bank balance should be

A    £5,100 overdrawn

B    £6,000 overdrawn

C    £6,250 overdrawn

D    £6,450 overdrawn

LO 2b

23  Which TWO of the following statements about bank reconciliations are correct?

A    In preparing a bank reconciliation, unpresented cheques must be deducted from a balance of cash at bank shown in the bank statement.

B    A cheque from a customer paid into the bank but dishonoured must be corrected by making a debit entry in the cash book.

C    An error by the bank must be corrected by an entry in the cash book.

D    An overdraft is a debit balance in the bank statement.

E    Bank charges that only appear on the bank statement must be debited in the cash book.

LO 2b

24   The trial balance of Delta Ltd did not agree and a suspense account was opened for the difference. Which TWO of the following errors found would require an entry to the suspense account as part of the process of correcting them?

   A   A cash refund to a customer was correctly treated in the cash book and then credited to the receivables control account

   B   The sale of goods to an employee for £300 was recorded by debiting sales and crediting payables

   C   The discount received column total in the cash book had been credited in error to the discount allowed account

   D   Some cash received from customers had been used to pay sundry expenses. It was debited to expenses and credited to the cash book

   E   £5,800 paid for plant repairs was correctly treated in the cash book and then credited to plant and equipment asset account

LO 2b

25   Alpha received a statement from its supplier Beta, showing a balance to be paid of £8,950. Alpha's payables ledger account for Beta shows a balance due to Beta of £4,140.

   Investigation reveals the following:

   1   Cash paid to Beta £4,080 has not been recorded by Beta.

   2   Alpha has not adjusted the ledger account for £40 of cash discount disallowed by Beta.

   3   Goods returned by Alpha £380 have not been recorded by Beta.

   What discrepancy remains between Alpha's and Beta's records after allowing for these items?

   A   £9,310

   B   £390

   C   £310

   D   £1,070

LO 2a

26   A bank statement on 31 October 20X7 showed an overdraft of £800. On reconciling the bank statement, it was discovered that a cheque drawn for £80 had not been presented for payment, and that a cheque for £130 from a customer had been dishonoured on 30 October 20X7, but this had not yet been reflected in the cash book.

   The correct bank balance to be shown in the statement of financial position at 31 October 20X7 is

   A   £1,010 overdrawn

   B   £880 overdrawn

   C   £750 overdrawn

   D   £720 overdrawn

LO 2b

27 Peri's bookkeeper made the following mistakes:

1    Discount allowed £3,840 was credited to discounts received account.

2    Discount received £2,960 was debited to discounts allowed account.

3    Discounts were otherwise correctly recorded.

Which of the following journal entries will correct the errors?

A    Debit Discount allowed £7,680, Credit Discount received £5,920, Credit Suspense account £1,760

B    Debit Discount allowed £880, Debit Discount received £880, Credit Suspense account £1,760

C    Debit Discount allowed £6,800, Credit Discount received £6,800

D    Debit Discount allowed £3,840, Credit Discount received £2,960, Credit Suspense account £880

LO 2d

28 The payables control account below contains a number of errors:

PAYABLES CONTROL ACCOUNT

| | £ | | £ |
|---|---|---|---|
| Opening balance (amounts owed to suppliers) | 318,600 | Purchases | 1,268,600 |
| Cash paid to suppliers | 1,405,500 | Contras against debit balances in receivables ledger | 48,000 |
| | | Discounts received | 8,200 |
| Refunds received from suppliers | 2,700 | Closing balance | 402,000 |
| | 1,726,800 | | 1,726,800 |

All items relate to credit purchases.

What should the closing balance be when all the errors are corrected?

A    £128,200

B    £122,800

C    £224,200

D    £144,600

LO 2b

29 A receivables control account had a closing balance of £8,500. It contained a contra to the payables ledger of £400, but this had been entered on the wrong side of the control account.

The correct debit balance on the control account is

A    £7,700

B    £8,100

C    £9,300

D    £8,900

LO 2b

30  Your firm's cash book at 30 April 20X8 shows a balance at the bank of £2,490. Comparison with the bank statement at the same date reveals the following differences:

|  | £ |
|---|---|
| Unpresented cheques | 840 |
| Bank charges not in cash book | 50 |
| Receipts not yet credited by the bank | 470 |
| Dishonoured cheque not adjusted in cash book | 140 |

The correct cash book balance at 30 April 20X8 is

A  £1,930

B  £2,300

C  £2,580

D  £3,140

LO 2b

31  The following receivables control account has been prepared:

### RECEIVABLES CONTROL ACCOUNT

| 20X5 |  | £ | 20X5 |  | £ |
|---|---|---|---|---|---|
| 1 Jan | Balance | 318,650 | 31 Jan | Cash from credit customers | 181,140 |
| 31 Jan | Credit sales | 157,780 |  | Refunds to credit customers | 280 |
|  | Cash sales | 84,260 |  | Irrecoverable debts written off | 1,390 |
|  | Discounts allowed |  |  |  |  |
|  | to credit customers | 1,240 |  |  |  |
|  |  |  |  | Balance | 379,120 |
|  |  | 561,930 |  |  | 561,930 |

What should the closing balance at 31 January 20X5 be after correcting the errors in the account?

A  £292,380

B  £295,420

C  £292,940

D  £295,720

LO 2b

32 The following receivables control account has been prepared:

RECEIVABLES CONTROL ACCOUNT

| | £ | | £ |
|---|---|---|---|
| Opening balance | 180,000 | Credit sales | 182,000 |
| Cash from credit customers | 228,000 | Irrecoverable debts written off | 1,500 |
| Cash refunds to credit customers | 3,300 | Contras against payables | 2,400 |
| Discount allowed | 4,200 | Closing balance | 229,600 |
| | 415,500 | | 415,500 |

What should the closing balance be after correcting the errors made in preparing the account?

A    £130,600

B    £129,200

C    £142,400

D    £214,600

LO 2b

33 Which THREE of the following differences between a company's cash book balance and its bank statement balance as at 30 November 20X3 would feature in the bank reconciliation statement:

A    Cheques recorded and sent to suppliers before 30 November 20X3 but not yet presented for payment

B    Omission by the bank of a lodgement made by the company on 26 November 20X3

C    Bank charges

D    Cheques paid in before 30 November 20X3 but not credited by the bank until 3 December 20X3

E    A customer's cheque recorded and paid in before 30 November 20X3 but dishonoured by the bank

LO 2b

34 In performing a bank reconciliation exercise, which TWO of the following require an entry in the cash book?

A    Cheque paid in, subsequently dishonoured on the bank statement

B    Error by bank

C    Bank charges

D    Lodgements credited after date

E    Outstanding cheques not yet presented

LO 2b

35 In preparing a company's bank reconciliation statement at 31 March 20X3, which THREE of the following items would give rise to amendments to the cash book?

A Bank charges £380

B Error by bank £1,000 (cheque incorrectly debited to the account)

C Lodgements not credited £4,580

D Outstanding cheques £1,475

E Direct debit payment £350

F Cheque paid in by the company and dishonoured £400

LO 2b

36 Two errors have been found in Trim plc's accounts:

I The credit balance of £420 in Ahmed's payables ledger account had been set off against his account in the receivables ledger, but no entries had been made in the receivables and payables control accounts.

2 Thomas' personal account balance of £240 had been removed from the receivables ledger as an irrecoverable debt, but no entry had been made in the receivables control account.

The journal that corrects both these errors is

A Debit Payables control £420, Debit Irrecoverable debts expense £240, Credit Receivables control £660

B Debit Receivables control £660, Credit Irrecoverable debts expense £240, Credit Payables control £420

C Debit Payables control £660, Credit Irrecoverable debts expense £240, Credit Receivables control £420

D Debit Receivables control £420, Debit Irrecoverable debts expense £240, Credit Payables control £660

LO 2d

37  P & Co maintain a receivables control account in the nominal ledger. At 30 November 20X0, the total of the list of individual balances extracted from the receivables ledger was £15,800, which did not agree with the balance on the receivables control account. An examination of the books revealed the following information, which can be used to reconcile the receivables ledger and the receivables control account.

1    The personal account of Mahmood was undercast by £90.

2    Yasmin's balance of (debit) £780 had been omitted from the list of balances.

3    The January total of £8,900 in the sales daybook had been posted as £9,800.

4    A credit note to Charles for £1,000, plus VAT of £200, had been posted to the receivables control account as £1,200 and to Charles' personal account as £1,000.

5    The total on the credit side of Edward's personal account had been overcast by £150.

What is the revised total of the balances in the receivables ledger after the errors have been corrected?

A    £17,020

B    £16,620

C    £16,440

D    £16,320

LO 2b

38  An error of principle would occur if plant and machinery purchased

A    Was credited to a non-current assets account

B    Was debited to the purchases account

C    Was debited to the equipment account

D    Was debited to the correct account but with the wrong amount

LO 2a

39  The balance on Janet's cash book is £27 overdrawn. Her bank statement shows that she is £625 in credit. When Janet does a reconciliation she finds that there are unpresented cheques of £327, unposted direct debits of £200, and a customer has paid £525 directly into her bank account. Her cash book should have a debit balance of

A    £298

B    £352

C    £752

D    £952

LO 2b

40 Which of the following statements about bank reconciliations are correct?

    1    All differences between the cash book and the bank statement must be corrected by means of a journal entry.

    2    In preparing a bank reconciliation, lodgements recorded before date in the cash book but credited by the bank after date should reduce an overdrawn balance in the bank statement.

    3    Bank charges not yet entered in the cash book should be dealt with by an adjustment to the balance per the bank statement.

    4    If a cheque received from a customer is dishonoured after date, a credit entry in the cash book is required.

    A    2 and 4

    B    1 and 4

    C    2 and 3

    D    1 and 3

LO 2b

---

41 A suspense account was opened when a trial balance failed to agree. The following errors were later discovered.

    1    A gas bill of £420 had been recorded in the power expense account as £240

    2    A discount of £50 given to a customer had been credited to discounts received

    3    Interest received of £70 had been entered in the bank account only

The original balance on the suspense account was

    A    Debit £210

    B    Credit £210

    C    Debit £160

    D    Credit £160

LO 2b

---

42 The following payables control account contains some errors. All goods are purchased on credit.

PAYABLES CONTROL ACCOUNT

| | £ | | £ |
|---|---|---|---|
| Purchases | 945,800 | Opening balance | 384,600 |
| | | Cash paid to suppliers | 988,400 |
| Discounts received | 12,600 | | |
| Contras with receivables ledger | 4,200 | | |
| Closing balance | 410,400 | | |
| | 1,373,000 | | 1,373,000 |

What should the closing balance be when the errors have been corrected?

    A    £325,200

    B    £350,400

    C    £333,600

    D    £410,400

LO 2b

43  The following bank reconciliation statement has been partially completed for a company:

|                                          | £      |
|------------------------------------------|--------|
| Overdraft per bank statement             | 39,800 |
| Deposits credited after date             | 64,100 |
| Outstanding cheques presented after date | 44,200 |

The credit balance in the cash book should be

A    £148,100

B    £19,900

C    £68,500

D    £59,700

LO 2b

44  An error of commission is one where

A    A transaction has not been recorded

B    One side of a transaction has been recorded in the wrong account, and that account is of a different class to the correct account

C    One side of a transaction has been recorded in the wrong account, and that account is of the same class as the correct account

D    A transaction has been recorded using the wrong amount

LO 2a

45  A company's bank statement shows an overdraft of £3,204 at 31 March 20X7. The statement includes bank charges of £46 which have not yet been recorded in the company's cash book. The statement does not include cheques for £780 paid to suppliers, nor an amount of £370 received from a credit customer; both of these amounts appear in the bank statement for April 20X7.

If the company prepares a statement of financial position at 31 March 20X7, the figure for the bank overdraft should be

A    £2,794

B    £3,568

C    £3,614

D    £3,660

LO 2b

46  Which of the following is an error in only the receivables ledger, not the control account?

A    Invoice omitted from the sales day book

B    Transposition error in posting to the receivables ledger from the sales day book

C    Transposition error in filling in the sales day book from an invoice sent out

D    Miscasting the total of the sales day book

LO 2a

47    A receivables ledger reconciliation was prepared by the bookkeeper of Corduroy and Co as at
      31 March 20X7 but one heading was illegible and has been called 'other difference'.

RECEIVABLES CONTROL ACCOUNT

|                          | £       |                          | £       |
|--------------------------|---------|--------------------------|---------|
| 31.3.07 Balance b/d      | 25,320  | Sales day book overcast  | 1,000   |
|                          |         | Balance c/d              | 24,320  |
|                          | 25,320  |                          | 25,320  |

|                                      | £       |
|--------------------------------------|---------|
| Total per receivables ledger listing | 23,890  |
| Credit balance listed as debit       | (280)   |
| 'Other difference'                   | 710     |
|                                      | 24,320  |

The 'other difference' is most likely to be:

A    Contra settlement omitted from the memorandum ledgers

B    Invoice omitted from the sales day book

C    Balance omitted from the receivables ledger listing

D    Irrecoverable debt not written off in the memorandum ledger

                                                                                        LO 2b


48    An error is identified where a discount received of £1,420 has been debited to both the payables
      control account and the discounts received account.

      The journal required to correct this is

A    Debit Suspense £2,840, Credit Discount received £2,840

B    Debit Suspense £1,420, Credit Discount received £1,420

C    Debit Suspense £2,840, Credit Payables control £2,840

D    Debit Suspense £1,420, Credit Payables control £1,420

                                                                                        LO 2d


49    Identify whether the following occurrences might explain the existence of a credit balance on a
      customer's receivables ledger account.

      The bookkeeper posted a total from the sales day book to the receivables control account twice by
      mistake.

A    Would explain a credit balance

B    Would not explain a credit balance

      The customer failed to take account of a credit note when paying an invoice.

C    Would explain a credit balance

D    Would not explain a credit balance

                                                                                        LO 2a

50   All Elmo's sales and purchases carry VAT at 20%. A customer has just returned goods sold for £230 plus VAT. The double entry for this transaction is

A   Debit Receivables control £276, Credit VAT control £46, Credit Sales £230

B   Debit Sales £276, Credit Receivables control £276

C   Debit Sales £230, Debit VAT control £46, Credit Receivables control £276

D   Debit Receivables control £230, Debit VAT control £46, Credit Sales £276

LO 2d

51   A supplier sends you a statement showing a balance outstanding of £14,350. Your own records show a balance outstanding of £14,500.

The reason for this difference could be that

A   The supplier sent an invoice for £150 which you have not yet received

B   The supplier has allowed you £150 cash discount which you omitted to enter in your ledgers

C   You have paid the supplier £150 which he has not yet accounted for

D   You have returned goods worth £150 which the supplier has not yet accounted for

LO 2a

52   Recording the purchase of computer stationery by debiting the computer equipment account would result in

A   An overstatement of profit and an overstatement of non-current assets

B   An understatement of profit and an overstatement of non-current assets

C   An overstatement of profit and an understatement of non-current assets

D   An understatement of profit and an understatement of non-current assets

LO 2a

53   Magma plc only buys inventories on credit.  At the end of May 20X4 the payables control account and the list of payables ledger balances fail to agree.

An invoice of £807 from Ferdinand has been recorded as a credit note in the purchase day book. In the payables control account reconciliation both the control account balance and the list of balances should be

A   Reduced by £807

B   Reduced by £1,614

C   Increased by £807

D   Increased by £1,614

LO 2b

54  Huskind plc only buys inventories on credit. At the end of October 20X1 the payables control account and the list of payables ledger balances fail to agree.

A discount allowed from Irina of £49 has been omitted from her ledger account, but has been recorded twice in the control account. In the payables control account reconciliation

A  Both the control account balance and the list of balances should be reduced by £49

B  The control account balance should be increased by £49 and the list of balances should be reduced by £49

C  The control account balance should be reduced by £49 and the list of balances should be increased by £49

D  Both the control account balance and the list of balances should be increased by £49

LO 2b

55  Which of the following statements about the trial balance is true?

A  A balanced trial balance means that transactions have been entered correctly into the ledger accounts

B  The trial balance is part of the nominal ledger

C  A suspense account with a credit balance means that the total of credit balances on the trial balance initially exceeded the total of debit balances

D  A trial balance may be used as the basis to produce an income statement and statement of financial position

LO 1e

56  Identify whether or not each of the following errors would result in opening a suspense account for Ramp plc.

A discount received from Bernard had been debited to discounts allowed but was correctly treated in the payables control account

A  Suspense account opened

B  Suspense account not opened

Goods returned by Cranberry had been debited to Cranberry's account in the receivables ledger and to the receivables control account but had been correctly treated in the sales account

C  Suspense account opened

D  Suspense account not opened

LO 2a

57 Ewan, a sole trader, has taken goods valued at £1,800 for his own use. This has not been recorded in arriving at his draft reported profit figure. To record the drawings he must:

Adjust cost of sales

A    Debit £1,800

B    Credit £1,800

So his reported profit will

C    Increase

D    Decrease

LO 2a, 2d

58 Hywel plc's trial balance includes a total for all the receivables ledger accounts as listed out at the year end. The receivables ledger is part of the double entry system. The trial balance fails to agree and a suspense account is opened. The difference is due to the following errors in Hywel plc's ledger accounts:

1    The balance on Markham plc's receivables ledger account is £9,890. This is incorrectly recorded in the trial balance as £9,980

2    A discount allowed to Umberto of £33 was debited to his receivables ledger account

3    The sales account is overcast by £110

Three journals are drafted to correct these errors. Together these journals should

A    Credit the suspense account with £110

B    Debit the suspense account with £86

C    Credit the suspense account with £46

D    Debit the suspense account with £46

LO 2b, 2d

59 At the end of January 20X7 Rock plc's payables control account and its list of payables ledger balances fail to agree.

It is discovered that the total of the purchase day book for January has been recorded as £11,750. The correct figure is £17,150. In the payables control account reconciliation

A    The control account balance should be reduced by £5,400

B    The list of balances should be increased by £5,400

C    The control account balance should be increased by £5,400

D    The list of balances should be reduced by £5,400

LO 2b

60 At 31 October 20X7 Osba plc had a receivables control account with a balance of £381,255. This balance was £782 more than the total on its list of receivables balances at the same date. Correction of which of the following errors would, alone, reconcile the two balances?

    A    A cheque received from Ellie plc for £391 had been recorded on the debit side of Ellie plc's account. Correct entries were made in the nominal ledger

    B    The total column in the sales day book had been overcast by £782

    C    A customer returned some goods to Osba plc on 30 November 20X7. These had originally been invoiced at £782. Osba plc recorded a credit note in the sales day book which was debited to the customer's account

    D    An invoice to Plion plc for £391 had been recorded in the sales day book as a credit note

LO 2b

---

61 Dredge plc makes only statutory deductions from employees' pay, which are all paid to HMRC when due. In March 20X6 Dredge plc paid £18,538 to its employees by bank transfer. Gross pay for the month of £28,456 was debited to the salaries expense account, but a debit balance of £3,983 remained on the salaries control account. This balance represented:

    A    Employer's NIC which should be debited to the salaries expense account

    B    Employer's NIC which should be credited to the HMRC liability account

    C    Total PAYE and NIC owed to HMRC for March which should be debited to the salaries expense account

    D    PAYE and employees' NIC deducted from gross pay which should be debited to the salaries expense account

LO 2b

---

62 Limbo plc maintains its petty cash records using an imprest system. The total petty cash float is topped up monthly to £300. During the month of August the following expenses were paid from petty cash:

| | £ |
|---|---|
| Stationery | 36 |
| Tea and coffee | 60 |
| Stamps | 120 |

In error, the purchase of stamps was recorded as £12 and as a result a cheque for £108 was written to top up the petty cash float.

The error made will result in which of the following?

    A    An imbalance in the trial balance of £108 and the petty cash balance being £108 less than it should be

    B    An understatement of expenses of £108 and the petty cash balance being £192 less than it should be

    C    An understatement of expenses of £108 and the petty cash balance being £108 less than it should be

    D    An imbalance in the trial balance of £192 and the petty cash balance being £192 less than it should be

LO 2a

63  As at 31 December 20X4 Isambard plc's trial balance failed to balance and a suspense account was opened. When the following errors were discovered and then rectified, the suspense account balance was eliminated.

1   The debit side of the trial balance was undercast by £692

2   A cheque payment of £905 had been credited in the cash book but no other entry in respect of it had been made

What was the original balance on the suspense account?

A   £1,597 Debit

B   £213 Debit

C   £1,597 Credit

D   £213 Credit

LO 2b

64  The debit balance in Omar plc's cash book at the year end is £42,510. The following items appear in the bank reconciliation at the year end.

|  | £ |
|---|---|
| Unpresented cheques | 2,990 |
| Uncleared lodgements | 10,270 |

A customer's cheque for £2,470 was returned unpaid by the bank before the year end, but this return has not been recorded in the cash book.

What was the balance in hand shown by the bank statement?

A   £37,700

B   £47,320

C   £35,230

D   £32,760

LO 2b

65  Rochelle has a debit balance of £26 in Staint plc's payables ledger. Which of the following would, alone, explain this balance?

A   Staint plc paid an invoice for £26 even though Rochelle had issued a credit note in respect of it

B   Staint plc bought and paid for some goods for £26 which it then returned, but Rochelle has not yet issued a credit note

C   Staint plc received a credit note for £26 from Rochelle but posted it to the account of Nashalle

D   Staint plc paid a cheque to Rochelle for £53 in respect of an invoice for £79

LO 2a, 2b

66 Padraig's trial balance at 31 December 20X0 contains a suspense account with a credit balance. Padraig queried the following items on the debit side of the trial balance, which he thinks he may have entered on the wrong side:

1   Rental income              £589

2   Discounts allowed          £421

3   Bank overdraft             £667

There are no other errors.

What is the credit balance on Padraig's suspense account?

A   £2,020

B   £2,512

C   £3,354

D   £2,176

LO 2b

67 Nassar plc's trial balance contains a suspense account with a credit balance of £27. Correction of which of the following errors would, alone, clear the suspense account?

A   A cash receipt of £63 was recorded in receivables as £36

B   A bad debt of £36 was recorded in receivables as £63

C   A sale to a credit customer of £63 was recorded in receivables as £36

D   An amount owed to a credit supplier of £63 was recorded in purchases as £36

LO 2b

68 Catt plc has prepared a draft income statement at 31 May 20X1 which shows a gross profit of £99,500. Catt plc has now discovered that at both the beginning and the end of the period one line of inventory, the Sungsa, has been included at selling price: £1,240 at 31 May 20X1 and £3,720 at 1 April 20X0. The Sungsa is always sold at a mark-up of 25% by Catt plc.

After correcting this error (which is not regarded as material) Catt plc's gross profit for the year to 31 May 20X1 is

A   £99,996

B   £99,004

C   £98,880

D   £100,120

LO 2a

69 Mayo plc has prepared a draft income statement that shows a net profit of £75,000 for the year ended 30 April 20X5. Subsequently, the following matters have been discovered.

    1    A subscription notice for £1,000 was received in April 20X5 for the year to 30 April 20X6. As the subscription had increased significantly Mayo plc decided to pay it in two equal instalments. The first instalment was paid on 28 April 20X5 and posted from the cash book to administrative expenses. No other entries have been made.

    2    Goods that cost £400 and sold at a gross margin of 75% were returned by Dandy Ltd on 30 April 20X5, after the inventory count had taken place. No credit note was issued.

Once these matters have been dealt with Mayo plc's net profit for the year ended 30 April 20X5 will be:

A    £75,400

B    £74,300

C    £75,100

D    £75,700

LO 2a

70 Hood plc has drawn up draft financial statements as at 31 October 20X2, which show a draft net profit of £540,000 and a suspense account with a £3,570 credit balance. The following errors have now been discovered.

    1    Repair costs of £6,600 incurred on 1 November 20X1 were debited to fixtures and fittings. Hood plc depreciates fixtures and fittings at 25% per annum.

    2    Discount allowed of £1,785 was debited to trade receivables.

On correction of these errors Hood plc's net profit will be:

A    £535,050

B    £531,480

C    £533,265

D    £529,830

LO 2a

71 Nimbus plc has prepared draft financial statements for the year ending 30 June 20X0, following a physical inventory count. However, on further investigation it has been realised that, in a burglary at the company's warehouse in May 20X0, inventory at a cost of £18,000 was stolen. Nimbus plc has insurance which covers 40% of the cost of inventory stolen. The insurance company has agreed to pay in this instance but no money has yet been received. No accounting entries have been made in respect of the stolen inventory.

Correcting this matter will

A    Increase net profit by £7,200

B    Decrease net profit by £7,200

C    Increase net profit by £10,800

D    Decrease net profit by £10,800

LO 2a

72   Pargetter plc's list of payables balances as at 31 October 20X3 exceeds the balance on its payables control account by £484.

Which of the following errors, alone, explains this difference?

A   Discount received of £484 has been entered in the ledger but not the control account

B   The purchases day book has been overcast by £484

C   A credit balance of £242 on an account in the payables ledger has been treated as a debit balance

D   Two credit notes for £484 each have been recorded in the purchases day book but only one has been posted to the payables ledger

LO 2b

73   The balance on Babcock plc's receivables control account at 30 September 20X2 is different from the total on the list of receivables ledger balances.

Which TWO of the following could have contributed to the difference?

A   A contra of £30 for Parkey was only recorded in the receivables ledger

B   A cheque for £30 from Springtime plc was not recorded in the cash book

C   A cash discount of £20 offered to Quince was not taken up

D   A trade discount on an invoice to Apstis Ltd was calculated at £15 too low

E   A cash book total for receipts from customers was miscast by £15

LO 2b

74   Backroom plc correctly records £6,413 in hand as the bank balance in its statement of financial position at 31 March 20X3 after receiving the year-end bank statement. This shows interest credited of £126 which had not previously been recorded in the cash book. The company notes that payments of £2,113 and receipts of £657 have not yet appeared on the bank statement.

The bank statement shows a balance of

A   £4,957

B   £7,743

C   £7,995

D   £7,869

LO 2b

75 At 31 March 20X3 Daphne plc had a payables control account with a balance of £162,458. This balance was £1,460 more than the total on its list of payables ledger balances at the same date.

Correction of which of the following errors would, alone, reconcile the two?

A Daphne plc returned some goods to Shaggy plc on 28 March 20X3. These had originally been invoiced at £1,460. The relevant credit note was recorded twice in the purchase day book.

B An invoice from Zoinks plc for £730 had been recorded in the purchase day book correctly, but had been posted to the individual payables account as a credit note.

C A cheque paid to Scooby plc for £1,460 had been recorded on the debit side of Scrappy plc's account

D The purchase day book had been undercast by £1,460

LO 2b

76 On extraction of Edmund plc's initial trial balance a suspense account has been created. Further investigation reveals the following errors and omissions for the year ended 31 July 20X0.

1 A sales day book total column for one week included credit notes of £120 as invoices. The bookkeeper adjusted the sales account for this error but no adjustment has been made to the receivables control account.

2 Cash book receipts from customers of £75 have been debited to the payables control account. The correct entry was made in the cash book.

3 A total from the sales day book of £455 has been credited to the receivables control account and to the sales account.

Once these are corrected the suspense account balance is eliminated.

What was the suspense account balance on Edmund plc's initial trial balance?

A £640 credit

B £520 debit

C £520 credit

D £640 debit

LO 2b

77 At 31 December 20X4 the total of Blunt plc's payables ledger balances was £29,800, but this did not agree with the payables control account balance at that date. Correction of the following items subsequently completed the payables ledger reconciliation:

1 The payables ledger column in one page of the cash book had been totalled at £2,950. The correct total was £2,590.

2 A debit balance in the payables ledger of £153 had been listed as a credit balance.

What was the original balance on Blunt plc's control account, and what was the corrected balance?

A Original balance £29,854, corrected balance £29,494

B Original balance £30,466, corrected balance £30,106

C Original balance £29,134, corrected balance £29,494

D Original balance £29,746, corrected balance £30,106

LO 2b

78 Uvavu plc correctly records £5,234 as the cash and cash equivalents balance in its statement of financial position at 28 February 20X7 after performing a bank reconciliation at that date. The bank statement showed interest expense of £102 and a direct credit from a customer of £8,642 which had not initially been recorded in the cash book. On the bank reconciliation the bookkeeper includes unpresented cheques of £5,833 and uncleared lodgements of £4,467.

Before the reconciliation was performed:

A    the cash book balance was £3,306 credit and the bank statement balance was £6,600 credit

B    the cash book balance was £3,510 credit and the bank statement balance was £3,868 credit

C    the cash book balance was £3,306 credit and the bank statement balance was £3,868 credit

D    the cash book balance was £3,510 credit and the bank statement balance was £6,600 credit

LO 2b

---

79 At 31 May 20X0 Rewind plc had a receivables control account with a balance of £246,060. This balance was £1,024 less than the total on its list of receivables balances at the same date.

Correction of which of the following errors would, alone, reconcile the two?

A    A customer returned some goods to Rewind plc on 30 May 20X0. These had originally been invoiced at £1,024. Rewind plc recorded a credit note in the sales day book which was credited twice to the customer's account

B    A credit note to Glitter plc for £512 had been recorded in the sales day book as an invoice

C    The total column in the sales day book had been undercast by £1,024

D    A cheque received from Vole plc for £1,024 had been returned by the bank as unpaid. The dishonoured cheque was debited to the receivables control account but no entry was made in Vole plc's receivables ledger

LO 2b

---

80 The total of the balances in the receivables ledger of Spook plc at the year end is £417,923. This does not agree with the balance on the receivables ledger control account. The following errors are discovered.

1    A credit balance of £2,340 on the receivables ledger was omitted.

2    An amount of £882 was written off as an irrecoverable debt in the receivables ledger. No record was made in the control account.

3    One month's sales totalling £36,825 had been incorrectly posted from the sales day book as £38,625.

When these errors are corrected, the difference between the receivables ledger balances and the control account is eliminated.

What was the balance on Spook plc's receivables ledger control account BEFORE these errors were corrected?

A    £414,665

B    £416,501

C    £422,945

D    £418,265

LO 2b

81 Fall plc's trial balance as at the year end 30 April 20X6 has been prepared. A summarised version which has been entered on the extended trial balance is as follows:

| Extended trial balance | Trial balance (summary) | |
|---|---|---|
| | £ | £ |
| Profit after tax | | 457,890 |
| Total non-current and current assets | 2,965,621 | |
| Current and non-current liabilities | | 1,341,835 |
| Share capital | | 300,000 |
| Retained earnings | | 860,610 |
| Suspense | | 5,286 |
| | 2,965,621 | 2,965,621 |

It has now been discovered that a rental income of £2,643 was debited to profit.

When this error is corrected and the extended trial balance is completed the credit balance on the retained earnings account will be

A £452,604

B £463,176

C £1,313,214

D £1,323,786

LO 1c, 2c

82 The credit column total on Santi plc's initial trial balance exceeds the debit column total by £78 so a suspense account is opened. Adjustments are entered in the adjustments columns of the extended trial balance as follows: debits £144 and credits £173. None of these adjustments is entered in the suspense account.

What is the balance on the suspense account that remains to be cleared?

A £107 credit

B £107 debit

C £49 debit

D £49 credit

LO 2b, 2c

83 On reviewing its cash book and its latest bank statement, Probla plc discovers the following errors:

1  A cheque from a customer for £1,095 was recorded in the cash book as £1,509

2  A cheque to a credit supplier for £89 was entered correctly in the total column of the cash book but was analysed in its payables ledger column as £889

To correct these errors Probla plc should:

A Debit Suspense £800, Debit Receivables £414, Credit Payables £800, Credit Cash £414

B Debit Cash £386, Debit Receivables £414, Credit Payables £800

C Debit Payables £800, Credit Cash £386, Credit Receivables £414

D Debit Payables £800, Debit Cash £414, Credit Suspense £800, Credit Receivables £414

LO 2b

84  In relation to its payables control account, at its year end of 30 April 20X1 Jitka plc has discovered that:

1   A contra of £85 with the receivables control account is required

2   Discount allowed to customers of £2,220 during the year to 30 April 20X1 was credited to administrative expenses and debited to the payables control account

Before these discoveries the balance on the payables control account was £72,560. In its statement of financial position as at 30 April 20X1 Jitka plc will have a figure for trade and other payables of

A   £70,255

B   £74,695

C   £74,865

D   £76,915

LO 2a, 3c

85  In relation to its payables control account, at its year end of 30 April 20X1 Jitka plc has discovered that:

1   A contra of £85 with the receivables control account is required

2   Discount allowed to customers of £2,220 during the year to 30 April 20X1 was credited to administrative expenses and debited to the payables control account

Before these discoveries the balance on the administrative expenses account (including other discounts allowed) was £31,990.

In its income statement for the year to 30 April 20X1 Jitka plc will have a figure for administrative expenses of:

A   £27,550

B   £29,770

C   £34,210

D   £36,430

LO 2a, 3c

86  Topping plc's extended trial balance for the year ended 31 October 20X9 has been prepared. It shows draft profit after tax of £58,147 and a credit balance on a suspense account of £738. It has now been discovered that expenses of £738 should have been treated as accrued, but the only entry made was to debit £738 to prepayments before the extended trial balance was prepared.

What is Topping plc's profit after tax when this error is corrected and the extended trial balance is completed?

A   £59,623

B   £57,409

C   £58,885

D   £56,671

LO 2a, 2c

1    A business compiling its financial statements for the year to 31 October each year pays rent quarterly in advance on 1 January, 1 April, 1 July and 1 October each year. The annual rent was increased from £48,000 to £60,000 per year from 1 March 20X4.

What figure should appear for rent in the income statement for the year ended 31 October 20X4 and in the statement of financial position at that date?

|   | Income statement | Statement of financial position |
|---|---|---|
| A | £56,000 | £10,000 |
| B | £52,000 | £5,000 |
| C | £56,000 | £5,000 |
| D | £55,000 | £10,000 |

LO 1c, 3c

2    A business has received telephone bills as follows:

|   | Date received | Amount of bill £ | Date paid |
|---|---|---|---|
| Quarter to 30 November 20X0 | December 20X0 | 739.20 | January 20X1 |
| Quarter to 28 February 20X1 | March 20X1 | 798.00 | April 20X1 |
| Quarter to 31 May 20X1 | June 20X1 | 898.80 | June 20X1 |
| Quarter to 31 August 20X1 | September 20X1 | 814.80 | October 20X1 |
| Quarter to 30 November 20X1 | December 20X1 | 840.00 | January 20X2 |
| Quarter to 28 February 20X2 | March 20X2 | 966.00 | March 20X2 |

The telephone expense in the income statement for the year ended 31 December 20X1 should be

A    £3,407.60

B    £3,351.60

C    £3,250.80

D    £3,463.60

LO 1c, 3c

3   A company receives rent from a large number of properties. The total cash received in the year ended 31 October 20X6 was £481,200.

The following are the amounts of rent in advance and in arrears at 31 October 20X5 and 20X6.

|  | 31 October 20X5 £ | 31 October 20X6 £ |
|---|---|---|
| Rent received in advance | 28,700 | 31,200 |
| Rent in arrears (all subsequently received) | 21,200 | 18,400 |

What amount of rental income should appear in the company's income statement for the year ended 31 October 20X6?

A   £486,500

B   £460,900

C   £501,500

D   £475,900

LO 1c, 3c

4   A rent prepayment of £960 was treated as an accrual in a sole trader's income statement at the year end. As a result the profit was

A   Understated by £960

B   Understated by £1,920

C   Overstated by £1,920

D   Overstated by £960

LO 1c, 3c

5   In the year ended 31 December 20X4 B Ltd received cash of £318,600 from subscribers to its website.

Details of subscriptions in advance and in arrears at the beginning and end of 20X4 are as follows:

|  | 31 December | |
|---|---|---|
|  | 20X4 £ | 20X3 £ |
| Subscriptions received in advance | 28,400 | 24,600 |
| Subscriptions owing | 18,300 | 16,900 |

All subscriptions owing were subsequently received.

What figure for subscriptions income should be included in the income statement of B Ltd for 20X4?

A   £321,000

B   £336,400

C   £300,800

D   £316,200

LO 1c, 3c

6    A company receives rent for subletting part of its office block.

Rent, receivable quarterly in advance, is received as follows:

| Date of receipt | Period covered | £ |
|---|---|---|
| 1 October 20X1 | 3 months to  31 December 20X1 | 7,500 |
| 30 December 20X1 | 3 months to  31 March 20X2 | 7,500 |
| 4 April 20X2 | 3 months to  30 June 20X2 | 9,000 |
| 1 July 20X2 | 3 months to  30 September 20X2 | 9,000 |
| 1 October 20X2 | 3 months to  31 December 20X2 | 9,000 |

What figures, based on these receipts, should appear in the company's financial statements for the year ended 30 November 20X2?

|   | Income statement | Statement of financial position |
|---|---|---|
| A | £33,500 Debit | Accrued income (Dr) £6,000 |
| B | £33,500 Credit | Deferred income (Cr) £6,000 |
| C | £34,000 Credit | Deferred income (Cr) £3,000 |
| D | £34,000 Credit | Accrued income (Dr) £3,000 |

LO 1c, 3c

---

7    During 20X4, B paid a total of £60,000 for rent, covering the period from 1 October 20X3 to 31 March 20X5.

What figures should appear in the  financial statements for the year ended 31 December 20X4?

|   | Income statement | Statement of financial position |
|---|---|---|
| A | £40,000 | £10,000 Prepayment |
| B | £40,000 | £15,000 Prepayment |
| C | £50,000 | £10,000 Accrual |
| D | £50,000 | £15,000 Accrual |

LO 1c, 3c

---

8    A company pays rent quarterly in arrears on 1 January, 1 April, 1 July and 1 October each year. The rent was increased from £90,000 per year to £120,000 per year as from 1 October 20X2.

What rent expense and accrual should be included in the company's financial statements for the year ended 31 January 20X3?

|   | Rent expense | Accrual |
|---|---|---|
| A | £100,000 | £20,000 |
| B | £100,000 | £10,000 |
| C | £97,500 | £10,000 |
| D | £97,500 | £20,000 |

LO 1c, 3c

9   A company owns a number of properties which are rented to tenants. The following information is available for the year ended 30 June 20X6:

|  | Rent in advance £ | Rent in arrears £ |
|---|---|---|
| 30 June 20X5 | 134,600 | 4,800 |
| 30 June 20X6 | 144,400 | 8,700 |

Cash received from tenants in the year ended 30 June 20X6 was £834,600.

All rent in arrears was subsequently received.

What figure should appear in the company's income statement for rent receivable in the year ended 30 June 20X6?

A   £840,500

B   £1,100,100

C   £569,100

D   £828,700

LO 1c, 3c

10  A company has sublet part of its offices and in the year ended 30 November 20X3 the rent receivable was:

| Until 30 June 20X3 | £8,400 per year |
|---|---|
| From 1 July 20X3 | £12,000 per year |

Rent was received quarterly in advance on 1 January, April, July, and October each year.

What amounts should appear in the company's financial statements for the year ended 30 November 20X3?

|  | Income statement rent receivable | Statement of financial position |
|---|---|---|
| A | £9,900 | £2,000 in other payables |
| B | £9,900 | £1,000 in other payables |
| C | £9,600 | £1,000 in other payables |
| D | £9,600 | £2,000 in other receivables |

LO 1c, 3c

11  A business compiling its financial statements for the year to 31 July each year pays rent quarterly in advance on 1 January, 1 April, 1 July and 1 October each year. The annual rent was increased from £60,000 per year to £72,000 per year as from 1 October 20X3.

What figure should appear for rent expense in the income statement for the year ended 31 July 20X4?

A   £69,000

B   £62,000

C   £70,000

D   £63,000

LO 1c, 3c

12   At 1 July 20X4 a company had prepaid insurance of £8,200. On 1 January 20X5 the company paid £38,000 for insurance for the year to 30 September 20X5.

What figures should appear for insurance in the company's financial statements for the year ended 30 June 20X5?

|   | Income statement | Statement of financial position |
|---|---|---|
| A | £45,200 | Prepayment £0 |
| B | £39,300 | Prepayment £9,500 |
| C | £36,700 | Prepayment £9,500 |
| D | £39,300 | Prepayment £0 |

LO 1c, 3c

13   A company sublets part of its office accommodation. In the year ended 30 June 20X5 cash received from tenants was £83,700.

Details of rent in arrears and in advance at the beginning and end of the year were:

|   | In arrears £ | In advance £ |
|---|---|---|
| 30 June 20X4 | 3,800 | 2,400 |
| 30 June 20X5 | 4,700 | 3,000 |

All arrears of rent were subsequently received.

What figure for rental income should be included in the company's income statement for the year ended 30 June 20X5?

A   £84,000

B   £83,400

C   £80,600

D   £86,800

LO 1c, 3c

14   Details of a company's insurance policy are shown below

| Premium for year ended 31 March 20X6 paid April 20X5 | £10,800 |
|---|---|
| Premium for year ending 31 March 20X7 paid April 20X6 | £12,000 |

What figures should be included in the company's financial statements for the year ended 30 June 20X6?

|   | Income statement | Statement of financial position |
|---|---|---|
| A | £11,100 | £9,000 prepayment (Dr) |
| B | £11,700 | £9,000 prepayment (Dr) |
| C | £11,100 | £9,000 accrual (Cr) |
| D | £11,700 | £9,000 accrual (Cr) |

LO 1c, 3c

15  An organisation's year end is 30 September. On 1 January 20X6 the organisation took out a loan of £100,000 with annual interest of 12%. The interest is payable in equal instalments on the first day of April, July, October and January in arrears.

How much should be charged to the income statement for the year ended 30 September 20X6, and how much should be accrued on the statement of financial position?

|   | Income statement | Statement of financial position |
|---|---|---|
| A | £12,000 | £3,000 |
| B | £9,000 | £3,000 |
| C | £9,000 | £0 |
| D | £6,000 | £3,000 |

LO 1c, 3c

16  A business sublets part of its office accommodation.

The rent is received quarterly in advance on 1 January, 1 April, 1 July and 1 October. The annual rent has been £24,000 for some years, but it was increased to £30,000 from 1 July 20X5.

What amounts for this rent should appear in the company's financial statements for the year ended 31 January 20X6?

|   | Income statement | Statement of financial position |
|---|---|---|
| A | £27,500 | £5,000 accrued income |
| B | £27,000 | £2,500 accrued income |
| C | £27,000 | £2,500 deferred income |
| D | £27,500 | £5,000 deferred income |

LO 1c, 3c

17  The electricity account for the year ended 30 June 20X1 was as follows.

|   | £ |
|---|---|
| Opening balance for electricity accrued at 1 July 20X0 | 300 |
| Payments made during the year | |
| 1 August 20X0 for three months to 31 July 20X0 | 600 |
| 1 November 20X0 for three months to 31 October 20X0 | 720 |
| 1 February 20X1 for three months to 31 January 20X1 | 900 |
| 30 June 20X1 for three months to 30 April 20X1 | 840 |

On 1 August 20X1 a payment of £840 was made for the three months ended 31 July 20X1.

The charge for electricity in the income statement for the year ended 30 June 20X1 is

A   £3,060

B   £3,320

C   £3,360

D   £3,620

LO 1c, 3c

18  The year end of M plc is 30 November 20X1. The company pays for its gas by a standing order of £600 per month. On 1 December 20X0, the statement from the gas supplier showed that M plc had overpaid by £200. M plc received gas bills for the four quarters commencing on 1 December 20X0 and ending on 30 November 20X1 for £1,300, £1,400, £2,100 and £2,000 respectively.

Calculate the correct charge for gas in M plc's income statement for the year ended 30 November 20X1.

A   £6,600

B   £6,800

C   £7,200

D   £7,400

LO 1c, 3c

---

19  At 31.12.20X8 Blue Anchor plc has an insurance prepayment of £250. During 20X9 they pay £800 in respect of various insurance contracts. The closing accrual for insurance is £90.

The income statement charge for insurance for the year ended 31.12.20X9 is

A   £460

B   £800

C   £960

D   £1,140

LO 1c, 3c

---

20  At 31 March 20X7, accrued rent payable was £300. During the year ended 31 March 20X8, rent paid was £4,000, including an invoice for £1,200 for the quarter ended 30 April 20X8.

What is the income statement charge for rent payable for the year ended 31 March 20X8?

A   £3,300

B   £3,900

C   £4,100

D   £4,700

LO 1c, 3c

---

21  Constains plc has an insurance prepayment of £320 at 31 March 20X2. During the year ended 31 March 20X2 Constains paid two insurance bills, one for £1,300 and one for £520.

The charge for the year in the accounts for insurance was £1,760. The prepayment at 31 March 20X1 was

A   £200

B   £260

C   £320

D   £380

LO 1c, 3c

22  The annual insurance premium for B Ltd for the period 1 July 20X6 to 30 June 20X7 is £13,200, which is 10% more than the previous year. Insurance premiums are paid on 1 July.

The income statement charge for insurance for the year ended 31 December 20X6 is

A    £12,000

B    £12,600

C    £13,200

D    £14,520

LO 1c, 3c

23  A gas accrual for £400 at the year end was treated as a prepayment in a business's income statement.

As a result the profit was

A    Understated by £400

B    Overstated by £400

C    Understated by £800

D    Overstated by £800

LO 2a

24  At 31 December 20X2 the following matters require inclusion in a company's financial statements:

1    On 1 January 20X2 the company made a loan of £12,000 to an employee, repayable on 30 April 20X3, charging interest at 2% per year. On the due date she repaid the loan and paid the whole of the interest due on the loan to that date.

2    The company has paid insurance £9,000 in 20X2, covering the year ending 31 August 20X3.

3    In January 20X3 the company received rent from a tenant £4,000 covering the six months to 31 December 20X2.

For these items, what total figures should be included in the company's statement of financial position at 31 December 20X2?

| | Current assets | Current liabilities |
|---|---|---|
| A | £22,000 | £240 |
| B | £22,240 | £0 |
| C | £10,240 | £0 |
| D | £16,240 | £6,000 |

LO 1c, 3c

25  On 1 April 20X6 a business paid £2,860 in local property tax for the year ending 31 March 20X7. This was an increase of 10% on the charge for the previous year.

The correct charge for local property tax in the income statement for the year ended 31 December 20X6 is

A    £2,665

B    £2,730

C    £2,795

D    £2,860

LO 1c, 3c

26  A business has opening inventory of £7,200 and closing inventory of £8,100. Purchases for the year were £76,500, carriage inwards was £50 and carriage outwards was £180.

The figure for cost of sales is

A    £75,550

B    £75,650

C    £75,830

D    £77,450

LO 1c, 3c

27  Whilst preparing the extended trial balance for a business it was determined that an accrual for electricity was required for £300 and that there was a prepayment of insurance of £800.

What four entries are required in the adjustments column of the extended trial balance?

A    Debit electricity              £300

B    Debit insurance               £800

C    Credit electricity            £300

D    Credit insurance              £800

E    Debit accruals                £300

F    Credit accruals               £300

G    Debit prepayments             £800

H    Credit prepayments            £800

LO 1c, 2c

28  A business has an accrual for electricity at 1 January 20X7 of £215 and has paid electricity bills of £3,420 during the year to 31 December 20X7. At 31 December 20X7 there is an accrual for electricity of £310.

The electricity charge in the income statement for the year ended 31 December 20X7 is

A  £2,895

B  £3,325

C  £3,515

D  £3,945

LO 1c, 3c

29  A business has paid £10,400 of insurance premiums during the year ended 31 March 20X7. At 1 April 20X6 there was an insurance prepayment of £800 and at 31 March 20X7 there was a prepayment of £920.

The insurance charge in the income statement for the year ended 31 March 20X7 is

A  £8,680

B  £10,280

C  £10,400

D  £10,520

LO 1c, 3c

30  Wright & Co's initial trial balance as at 31 August 20X4 has already been entered on the extended trial balance for the period.  Telephone line rental of £120 was paid on 31 July for the two months from that date.  In the adjustments columns on the extended trial balance Wright & Co should make TWO entries of £60:

A  Debit the telephone charges account

B  Debit the prepayments account

C  Debit the accruals account

D  Credit the accruals account

E  Credit the prepayments account

F  Credit the telephone charges account

LO 1c, 2c

31   Bark plc's initial trial balance as at 30 June 20X8 has already been entered on the extended trial balance for the period.  In respect of revenues in the year of £17,550, sales commission of 10% has not yet been paid.  In the adjustments columns on the extended trial balance Bark plc should make TWO entries of £1,755:

A   Debit the accruals account

B   Debit the prepayments account

C   Debit the distribution costs account

D   Credit the distribution costs account

E   Credit the prepayments account

F   Credit the accruals account

LO 1c, 2c

32   Krim plc paid local property tax of £6,495 on 31 May 20X7, in respect of the three months ending 31 August 20X7.  In the administrative expenses ledger account for the year ended 30 June 20X7 Krim plc must:

A   Debit £2,165

B   Credit £2,165

C   Debit £4,330

D   Credit £4,330

LO 1c

33   Gleeson plc has a year end of 30 June 20X7.  An opening journal at 1 July 20X6 entered a prepayment of £215 as at 30 June 20X6 as an accrual in the administrative expenses account.  In this ledger account Gleeson plc must:

A   Debit £215

B   Credit £215

C   Debit £430

D   Credit £430

LO 2a, 2d

34  Jared plc is preparing its financial statements for the 12-month reporting period ended 30 June 20X9. Its initial trial balance includes:

 –   A balance for administrative expenses paid in the reporting period (including rent) of £44,064

 –   A balance for prepayment of rent at 1 July 20X8 of £4,251

On 31 May 20X9 Jared plc paid its quarterly rent in advance of £7,200.

In Jared plc's income statement for the year ended 30 June 20X9 the figure for administrative expenses will be

A    £35,013

B    £43,515

C    £44,064

D    £45,915

LO 3c

35  Platoon plc is preparing its financial statements for the year ended 30 April 20X1, having prepared an initial trial balance.

Purchases in the period were £686,880. Inventories were valued at £18,081 on 1 May 20X0, and at £18,647 on 30 April 20X1.  In Platoon plc's income statement for the year ended 30 April 20X1 the figure for cost of sales will be:

A    £686,314

B    £686,880

C    £687,446

D    £723,608

LO 3c

36  Muse plc commences trading on 1 January 20X8 and has zero inventories at that date. During 20X8 it has purchases of £455,000, incurs carriage inwards of £24,000, and carriage outwards of £29,000. Closing inventories at 31 December 20X8 are valued at £52,000.

In the income statement for the year ended 31 December 20X8 the cost of sales figure is:

A    £456,000

B    £427,000

C    £432,000

D    £531,000

LO 3c

37 Brindal plc acquired five apartments on 1 June 20X4 and immediately rented them out to different tenants. Brindal plc has a credit balance on its rent receivable account in its initial trial balance as at 31 May 20X5 of £22,850. In the adjustments column of the extended trial balance there are entries for rent in arrears as at 31 May 20X5 of £4,490, and for rent in advance at the same date of £7,720.

What amount will appear for rent under other income in Brindal plc's income statement for the year ended 31 May 20X5?

A    £19,620

B    £22,850

C    £26,080

D    £37,340

LO 2c, 3c

38 Iqbal plc is a newsagent business and is preparing its financial statements for the year ended 31 August 20X8. There are three outstanding matters that the company has not yet accounted for.

1    A subscription of £240 recorded as paid by Iqbal plc and accounted for on 1 July 20X8 for the year ending 31 January 20X9

2    Advance payments (deposits) of £75 recorded as received from customers in respect of magazines on order but not yet received at the year end

3    An unpaid property tax demand for the six months to 30 September 20X8 for £5,400

Which THREE of the following balances will appear in Iqbal plc's statement of financial position as at 31 August 20X8?

A    Deferred income £75

B    Accrued income £75

C    Prepayment £100

D    Accrual £4,500

E    Accrual £900

F    Prepayment £140

LO 1c, 3b, 3c

39 Minoto plc is preparing its financial statements as at 31 December 20X4. Its ledger account balance for rental income includes £9,870 rent received in 20X4 in respect of 20X3.

Minoto plc should enter a journal with two entries of £9,870 as

A    A debit entry to the rental income account

B    A debit entry to the deferred income (liability) account

C    A debit entry to the accrued income (asset) account

D    A credit entry to the rental income account

E    A credit entry to the deferred income (liability) account

F    A credit entry to the accrued income (asset) account

LO 1c, 2d, 3b

40  As at 30 November 20X4 Whitley plc had accrued distribution costs of £5,019 and prepaid distribution costs of £2,816. On 1 December 20X4 the bookkeeper processed the following opening journal: Credit Accruals £5,019, Debit Prepayments £2,816, Debit Distribution costs £2,203.

During the year to 30 November 20X5 cash was paid in respect of distribution costs of £147,049 and was correctly posted to the distribution costs account. At the year end, Whitley plc's bookkeeper correctly processed closing journals to set up an accrual of £4,423 and a prepayment of £3,324 in respect of distribution costs.

Which of the following journals should Whitley plc process as at 30 November 20X5 to correct the three accounts?

A   Debit Accruals £10,038, Credit Prepayments £5,632, Credit Distribution costs £4,406

B   Debit Accruals £5,019, Credit Prepayments £2,816, Credit Distribution costs £2,203

C   Debit Distribution costs £4,406, Debit Prepayments £5,632, Credit Accruals £10,038

D   Debit Distribution costs £2,203, Debit Prepayments £2,816, Credit Accruals £5,019

LO 1c, 2d, 3b

---

41  Bez plc draws up financial statements to 31 December in each year. It pays Internet server charges for each year ending 30 April in two equal instalments, on 1 May and 1 November, in advance. It also pays telephone rental charges quarterly in arrears at the end of February, April, July and November. The total Internet server charge for the year to 30 April 20X6 was £9,000. Telephone rental charges for the year commencing 1 July 20X5 were £7,440.

(a)  What was the prepayment for Internet server charges included in Bez plc's statement of financial position at 31 December 20X5?

A   £1,500

B   £3,000

C   £2,250

(b)  What was the accrual for telephone rental charges included in Bez plc's statement of financial position at 31 December 20X5?

D   £1,860

E   £1,240

F   £620

LO 1c, 3b, 3c

---

42  Butters plc is finalising certain figures that will appear in its financial statements as at 30 June 20X5. On 1 March 20X4 the company paid an annual fee to a trade association of £21,000 for the twelve months ended 28 February 20X5. A 12.5% increase in this subscription is expected, but has not been finalised at 30 June 20X5.

In its statement of financial position at 30 June 20X5 Butters plc will include

A   An accrual of £15,750

B   An accrual of £7,875

C   A prepayment of £15,750

D   A prepayment of £7,875

LO 1c, 3b, 3c

1    A company receives news that a major customer has been declared bankrupt. The amount he owed had been allowed for as doubtful earlier in the year. The journal now required is

A    Debit Allowance for receivables, Credit Receivables control

B    Debit Irrecoverable debts expense, Credit Receivables control

C    Debit Irrecoverable debts expense, Credit Allowance for receivables

D    Debit Allowance for receivables, Credit Irrecoverable debts expense

LO 1c, 2d

2    At 30 June 20X1 Cameron plc has decided to write off two debts of £1,300 and £2,150 respectively and to make a specific allowance for £6,631. The balance on this allowance at 1 July 20X0 was £8,540.

What is Cameron plc's irrecoverable debts expense for the year to 30 June 20X1?

A    £1,541

B    £1,909

C    £3,450

D    £5,359

LO 1c, 3c

3    Enigma plc has reduced its allowance for receivables by £600.

This will increase gross profit by £600

A    True

B    False

This will increase net profit by £600

C    True

D    False

LO 2a

4    Disaster plc's trial balance shows a receivables control account balance of £50,000. However, no adjustment has been made for the following items.

   1    £3,250 from J Crisis & Sons who have gone into liquidation. The amount is considered irrecoverable

   2    Debts of £500 and £1,500 which are to be specifically provided for

   3    Cash received from P Chaos of £2,500 which had previously been written off

   4    Cash received from T Ruin of £1,700 which had previously been provided for

   What is the revised trade receivables account balance after posting the above adjustments?

   A    £52,200

   B    £50,200

   C    £45,050

   D    £49,250

LO 1c, 3c

5    At 28 February 20X4, a company's allowance for receivables was £38,000. At 28 February 20X5 it was decided to write £28,500 off receivables and to make a specific allowance of £42,000.

   The income statement charge for the year ended 28 February 20X5 for irrecoverable debts is

   A    £42,000

   B    £28,500

   C    £70,500

   D    £32,500

LO 1c

6    Arrow plc had a receivables balance of £7,050 at 31 December 20X0. During the year £500 was received in respect of a debt previously written off, and a specific debt of £495 was provided for. The allowance brought down as at 1 January 20X0 was £1,000.

   In respect of irrecoverable debts for the year ended 31 December 20X0 Arrow plc will

   A    charge £5

   B    charge £1,005

   C    write back £5

   D    write back £1,005

LO 1c, 3c

7    The trial balance of Knight plc as at 31 May 20X0 includes an allowance for receivables of £2,050. Subsequently a review of the receivables ledger reveals that debts totalling £985 are considered irrecoverable and are to be written off. There is some doubt over the recoverability of another receivable, Carter Ltd, owing £2,157. The company wishes to make a specific allowance for this.

What irrecoverable debt expense will the income statement for the year ended 31 May 20X0 include?

A    £878

B    £985

C    £1,092

D    £2,157

LO 3c

8    During 20X5 Bow plc received £500 from a customer in respect of a balance that had previously been written off, and allowed for a debt of £100. The allowance brought down as at 1 January 20X5 was £1,000. At the year end the dishonour of a cheque received for £280 needs to be accounted for, and the debt related to it needs to be written off.

What is the irrecoverable debts debit or credit in the income statement for the year ended 31 December 20X5?

A    £880 debit

B    £780 debit

C    £1,120 credit

D    £1,300 credit

LO 3c

9    At 31 December 20X2 a company's receivables totalled £400,000 and an allowance for receivables of £50,000 had been brought forward from the year ended 31 December 20X1.

It was decided to write off debts totalling £38,000 and to adjust the allowance for receivables to £36,200.

What charge for irrecoverable debts should appear in the company's income statement for the year ended 31 December 20X2?

A    £36,200

B    £51,800

C    £38,000

D    £24,200

LO 3c

10   At 1 July 20X2 the receivables allowance of Q plc was £18,000.

During the year ended 30 June 20X3 debts totaling £14,600 were written off. It was decided that the receivables allowance should be £16,000 as at 30 June 20X3.

What amount should appear in Q plc's income statement for irrecoverable debts expense for the year ended 30 June 20X3?

A   £12,600

B   £14,600

C   £16,600

D   £30,600

LO 3c

---

11   The receivables ledger at 1 May had balances of £32,750 debit and £1,275 credit. During May, sales of £125,000 were made on credit. Receipts from receivables amounted to £122,500 and discounts of £550 were allowed. Refunds of £1,300 were made to customers. The net closing debit balance at 31 May on the receivables control account was

A   £34,725

B   £33,225

C   £32,125

D   £35,825

LO 1c

---

12   Panther plc had the following balances in its books at 30 June 20X2:

|  | £ |
|---|---|
| Receivables | 31,450 |
| Allowance for receivables (as at 1 July 20X1) | (450) |
|  | 31,000 |

Horrids Co was in financial difficulty and Panther plc wished to allow for 60% of their balance of £800, plus a further specific allowance of £2,965. What was the allowance for receivables in Panther plc's statement of financial position at 30 June 20X2?

A   £3,477

B   £3,765

C   £3,445

D   £3,545

LO 1c, 3c

13    The following receivables control account has been prepared by an inexperienced bookkeeper and
      may contain errors of principle.

                        RECEIVABLES CONTROL ACCOUNT

|        |                        | £       |        |                            | £       |
|--------|------------------------|---------|--------|----------------------------|---------|
| 20X3   |                        |         | 20X3   |                            |         |
| 1 Jan  | Balance                | 284,680 | 31 Dec | Cash received from credit  |         |
| 31 Dec | Credit sales           | 194,040 |        |   customers                | 179,790 |
|        | Discounts allowed      | 3,660   |        | Contras with payables ledger | 800   |
|        | Irrecoverable debts    |         |        | Balance                    | 303,590 |
|        | written off            | 1,800   |        |                            |         |
|        |                        | 484,180 |        |                            | 484,180 |

An outstanding debt of £4,920 at 31 December 20X3 is to be written off.

What is the correct figure for receivables that should appear on the statement of financial position
at 31 December 20X3?

A    £289,350

B    £291,350

C    £287,750

D    £297,590

LO 1c, 3c

14    At 30 June 20X4 a company's allowance for receivables was £39,000. At 30 June 20X5 trade
      receivables totalled £517,000. It was decided to write off debts totalling £37,000 and to adjust the
      allowance for receivables to £24,000.

What figure should appear in the income statement for irrecoverable debts expense for the year
ended 30 June 20X5?

A    £52,000

B    £22,000

C    £37,000

D    £23,850

LO 3c

15   At 1 January 20X5 a company had an allowance for receivables of £18,000.

At 31 December 20X5 the company's trade receivables were £458,000.

It was decided:

(a)   To write off debts totalling £28,000 as irrecoverable;

(b)   To adjust the allowance for receivables to £21,500.

What figure should appear in the company's income statement for irrecoverable debts expense for the year ended 31 December 20X5?

A   £49,500

B   £31,500

C   £32,900

D   £50,900

LO 3c

16   At 1 July 20X5 a company's allowance for receivables was £48,000.

At 30 June 20X6, receivables amounted to £838,000. It was decided to write off £72,000 of these debts and adjust the allowance for receivables to £60,000.

What are the final amounts for inclusion in the company's statement of financial position at 30 June 20X6?

|   | Receivables £ | Allowance for receivables £ | Net balance £ |
|---|---|---|---|
| A | 838,000 | 60,000 | 778,000 |
| B | 766,000 | 60,000 | 706,000 |
| C | 766,000 | 108,000 | 658,000 |
| D | 838,000 | 108,000 | 730,000 |

LO 3c

17   At 30 September 20X0 a company has receivables totalling £350,000 and an allowance for receivables of £22,000 brought forward from the previous year.

It has been decided to write off receivables totalling £27,500. An allowance of £22,575 is required at 30 September 20X0.

The total charge for irrecoverable debts in the company's income statement for the year ended 30 September 20X0 will be

A   £22,575

B   £26,925

C   £28,075

D   £50,075

LO 3c

18  If Poppy plc reduces its allowance for receivables by £300, which of the following statements is correct?

A   Current assets decrease by £300

B   Current liabilities decrease by £300

C   Gross profit increases by £300

D   Net profit increases by £300

LO 2a, 3c

19  At 31 December 20X4 a company's trade receivables totalled £864,000 and the allowance for receivables was £48,000.

It was decided that debts totalling £13,000 were to be written off, and the allowance for receivables adjusted to £42,550.

What figures should appear in the statement of financial position for net receivables (after deducting the allowance) and in the income statement for irrecoverable debts expense?

|   | Income statement Irrecoverable debts expense £ | Statement of financial position Net receivables £ |
|---|---|---|
| A | 7,550 | 803,000 |
| B | 7,550 | 808,450 |
| C | 18,450 | 808,450 |
| D | 13,000 | 803,000 |

LO 3c

20  A business has entered its initial trial balance as at 31 December 20X7 on the extended trial balance.

Extended trial balance (extract)

|   | Trial balance £ | £ |
|---|---|---|
| Trade receivables | 441,500 | |
| Allowance for receivables at 1 January 20X7 | | 20,300 |
| Irrecoverable debt expense | | |

A balance of £2,400 is to be written off as irrecoverable and the allowance for receivables is to be £21,955.

In the adjustments columns on the extended trial balance which THREE entries should be made?

A   A debit entry of £2,400 to trade receivables

B   A debit entry of £1,655 to allowance for receivables

C   A debit entry of £4,055 to irrecoverable debt expense

D   A credit entry of £2,400 to trade receivables

E   A credit entry of £1,655 to allowance for receivables

F   A credit entry of £4,055 to irrecoverable debt expense

LO 2c

21 Which THREE of the following items could appear on the credit side of a receivables control account?

A Cash received from customers

B Irrecoverable debts written off

C Increase in the allowance for receivables

D Discounts received

E Sales

F Credits for goods returned by customers

G Cash refunds to customers

LO 1c

22 At 1 January 20X1 Urb plc was owed £3,000 by Yakuk. Specific allowance had been made in full against Yakuk's balance at this date, but during 20X1 Yakuk paid off the debt.

At 31 December 20X1 Bobo's receivables balance in Urb plc's ledger accounts was £3,600, but Urb plc wishes to make full allowance against Bobo's balance.

Urb plc's income statement will include an irrecoverable debts figure for the year ended 31 December 20X1 of

A £600 debit

B £600 credit

C £3,600 debit

D £2,400 credit

LO 3c

23 At its year end of 28 February 20X6 Stope plc has in its draft financial statements a figure for trade receivables of £47,533, and an allowance for receivables in respect of Invincible plc of £500 at 28 February 20X5.

Invincible plc has worsening financial difficulties, and of its balance of £10,380 at 28 February 20X6, the directors of Stope plc expect to receive only 25% within one month. They wish to create an allowance for the remaining balance. They also identify an amount of £508 from Hup Ltd as being irrecoverable. In its completed financial statements as at 28 February 20X6 Stope plc will show

A Allowance for receivables of £500 and a charge in respect of irrecoverable debts of £8,293

B Allowance for receivables of £2,595 and a charge in respect of irrecoverable debts of £2,603

C Allowance for receivables of £7,785 and a charge in respect of irrecoverable debts of £7,793

D Allowance for receivables of £8,285 and a charge in respect of irrecoverable debts of £8,293

LO 3c

24 Moon plc's initial trial balance as at 31 October 20X1 has already been entered on the extended trial balance for the period.

Extended trial balance (extract)

| | Trial balance | |
|---|---|---|
| | £ | £ |
| Irrecoverable debt expense | | |
| Allowance for receivables as at 1 November 20X0 | | 6,546 |
| Trade receivables | 251,760 | |

As at 31 October 20X1 Grundle's balance to Moon plc of £1,860 is irrecoverable. Blenheim owes £12,650, but Moon plc believes an allowance of 40% of this amount is necessary. In the adjustments columns on the extended trial balance Moon plc should make THREE entries:

A   A debit entry of £374 to the irrecoverable debt expense account

B   A debit entry of £1,486 to the allowance for receivables account

C   A debit entry of £1,860 to the trade receivables account

D   A credit entry of £374 to the irrecoverable debt expense account

E   A credit entry of £1,486 to the allowance for receivables account

F   A credit entry of £1,860 to the trade receivables account

LO 2c, 3c

25 At its year end of 31 July 20X1 Hussar plc has in its draft financial statements a figure for trade receivables of £578,645, an allowance for receivables in respect of Cusack plc as at 1 August 20X0 of £1,200 and a charge for irrecoverable debts expense of £3,290. You are told that:

(1) Cusack plc's account was settled in full in the year

(2) an allowance of £250 is required against the account of Dancer plc

(3) a cheque for £89 was received at 31 July 20X1 in respect of an amount written off two years previously, but only the cash book has been updated for this

In its completed financial statements as at 31 July 20X1 Hussar plc will show:

A   Charge for irrecoverable debts of £2,251 and trade receivables net of allowance of £578,395

B   Charge for irrecoverable debts of £2,340 and trade receivables net of allowance of £577,606

C   Charge for irrecoverable debts of £2,340 and trade receivables net of allowance of £578,395

D   Charge for irrecoverable debts of £3,451 and trade receivables net of allowance of £578,395

LO 3c

26  Meridi plc has an allowance for irrecoverable debts of £500 on 1 July 20X7. During the year to 30 June 20X8 the following events take place:

   1   A cheque for £92 was recorded and correctly banked, but was returned unpaid on 29 June 20X8. No entries have yet been made for this return. The directors wish to write the debt off as irrecoverable.

   2   An allowance of £475 is required at the year end.

   3   A cheque received for £58 in respect of an amount written off in January 20X7 was recorded correctly in the cash book, but no other entry was made.

   What journal entries are required as at 30 June 20X8?

   A   Debit Cash £92, Credit Suspense £58, Credit Irrecoverable debts expense £9, Credit Allowance for irrecoverable debts £25

   B   Debit Suspense £58, Debit Receivables £92, Credit Irrecoverable debts expense £33, Credit Cash £92, Credit Allowance for irrecoverable debts £25

   C   Debit Suspense £58, Debit Irrecoverable debts expense £67, Debit Allowance for irrecoverable debts £25, Credit Cash £92, Credit Receivables £58

   D   Debit Suspense £58, Debit Irrecoverable debts expense £9, Debit Allowance for irrecoverable debts £25, Credit Cash £92

   LO 1c, 2d

---

27  At 1 January 20X5 Tandem plc had allowances in its ledger accounts in respect of two customers' debts: Basnet plc for £1,425 and Ost plc for £950. On 30 June 20X5 Basnet plc's liquidator informed Tandem plc that it would pay £200 only, so Tandem plc decided to write off the remainder of the balance. At 31 December 20X5 Ost plc had paid £500 of its debt outstanding at 31 December 20X4. Tandem plc wishes to maintain the allowance for the remainder of the balance.

   What is the figure for irrecoverable debts included in administrative expenses in Tandem plc's income statement for the year ended 31 December 20X5?

   A   £700 credit

   B   £650 credit

   C   £650 debit

   D   £700 debit

   LO 1c, 3c

# Chapter 9: Inventories

1   Boomerang Co had 200 units in inventory at 30 November 20X1 valued at £800. During December it made the following purchases and sales.

| | | | | |
|---|---|---|---|---|
| 2/12 | Purchased | 1,000 | @ | £5.00 each |
| 5/12 | Sold | 700 | @ | £7.50 each |
| 12/12 | Purchased | 800 | @ | £6.20 each |
| 15/12 | Purchased | 300 | @ | £6.60 each |
| 21/12 | Sold | 400 | @ | £8.00 each |
| 28/12 | Sold | 500 | @ | £8.20 each |

Which of the following is the closing inventory valuation using FIFO?

A   £4,460

B   £4,340

C   £4,620

D   £3,500

LO 1c

2   The following information relates to Camberwell plc's year-end inventory of finished goods.

| | Direct costs of materials and labour £ | Production overheads incurred £ | Expected selling and distribution overheads £ | Expected selling price £ |
|---|---|---|---|---|
| Inventories category 1 | 2,470 | 2,100 | 480 | 5,800 |
| Inventories category 2 | 9,360 | 2,730 | 150 | 12,040 |
| Inventories category 3 | 1,450 | 850 | 190 | 2,560 |
| | 13,280 | 5,680 | 820 | 20,400 |

At what amount should finished goods inventory be stated in the company's statement of financial position?

A   £13,280

B   £18,960

C   £18,760

D   £19,580

LO 1c

3    At its year end Crocodile plc has 6,000 items of product A, and 2,000 of product B, costing £10 and £5 respectively. The following information is available:

Product A – 500 are defective and can only be sold at £8 each.

Product B – 100 are to be sold for £4.50 each with selling expenses of £1.50 each.

What figure should appear in Crocodile plc's statement of financial position for inventory?

A    £57,000

B    £68,950

C    £68,800

D    £70,000

LO 1c, 3c

---

4    In a period of rising prices the FIFO method of charging inventory issues to production will give a lower gross profit figure than the AVCO method.

A    True

B    False

Closing inventory is a debit in the income statement.

C    True

D    False

LO 1c, 2a

---

5    Your firm values inventory using AVCO. At 1 June 20X8 there were 60 units in inventory valued at £12 each. On 8 June, 40 units were purchased for £15 each, and a further 50 units were purchased for £18 each on 14 June. On 21 June, 75 units were sold for £20.00 each.

The value of closing inventory at 30 June 20X8 was

A    £1,110

B    £1,010

C    £900

D    £1,125

LO 3c

---

6    For Morgan plc the direct production cost of each unit of inventory is £46. Production overheads are £15 per unit. Currently the goods can only be sold if they are modified at a cost of £17 per unit. The selling price of each modified unit is £80 and selling costs are estimated at 10% of selling price.

At what value should each unmodified unit of inventory be included in the statement of financial position?

A    £48

B    £55

C    £64

D    £61

LO 3c

---

7    A van for sale by a car dealer is shown as a non-current asset in its statement of financial position.

    A    True

    B    False

Import duties are included in the cost of inventory

    C    True

    D    False

LO 3c

8    Which TWO of the following may be included when arriving at the cost of finished goods inventory for inclusion in the financial statements of a manufacturing company?

    A    Carriage inwards

    B    Carriage outwards

    C    Depreciation of delivery vehicles

    D    Finished goods storage costs

    E    Production line wages

LO 1c

9    Which of the following statements about inventory valuation for the purposes of the statement of financial position is correct?

    A    AVCO and LIFO are both acceptable methods of arriving at the cost of inventories

    B    Inventories of finished goods may be valued at labour and materials cost only, without including overheads

    C    Inventories should be valued at the lowest of cost, net realisable value and replacement cost

    D    It may be acceptable for inventories to be valued at selling price less estimated profit margin

LO 1c

10   The closing inventory at cost of a company at 31 January 20X3 amounted to £284,700.

The following items were included at cost in the total:

    1    400 coats, which had cost £80 each and normally sold for £150 each. Owing to a defect in manufacture, they were all sold after 31 January 20X3 at 50% of their normal price. Selling expenses amounted to 5% of the proceeds.

    2    800 skirts, which had cost £20 each. These too were found to be defective. Remedial work in February 20X3 cost £5 per skirt, and selling expenses were £1 per skirt. They were sold for £28 each.

What should the inventory value be after considering the above items?

    A    £281,200

    B    £282,800

    C    £329,200

    D    £284,700

LO 1c

11  S plc sells three products – Basic, Super and Luxury. The following information was available at the year end.

|  | Basic £ per unit | Super £ per unit | Luxury £ per unit |
|---|---|---|---|
| Original cost | 6 | 9 | 18 |
| Estimated selling price | 9 | 12 | 15 |
| Selling and distribution costs to be incurred | 1 | 4 | 5 |
|  | units | units | units |
| Units of inventory | 200 | 250 | 150 |

The value of inventory at the year end should be

A    £3,600

B    £4,700

C    £5,100

D    £6,150

LO 1c

12  A company values its inventory using the FIFO method. At 1 May 20X2 the company had 700 engines in inventory, valued at £190 each.

During the year ended 30 April 20X3 the following transactions took place:

20X2
1 July                    Purchased 500 engines at £220 each
1 November          Sold 400 engines for £160,000
20X3
1 February            Purchased 300 engines at £230 each
15 April                Sold 250 engines for £125,000

What is the value of the company's closing inventory of engines at 30 April 20X3?

A    £188,500

B    £195,500

C    £161,500

D    £167,500

LO 1c

13  An inventory record card shows the following details.

| February | 1 | 50 units in inventory at a cost of £40 per unit |
| | 7 | 100 units purchased at a cost of £45 per unit |
| | 14 | 80 units sold |
| | 21 | 50 units purchased at a cost of £50 per unit |
| | 28 | 60 units sold |

What is the value of inventory at 28 February using the FIFO method?

A   £2,450

B   £2,500

C   £2,700

D   £2,950

LO 1c

14  For the year ended 31 October 20X3 a company did a physical check of inventory on 4 November 20X3, leading to an inventory value at cost at this date of £483,700.

Between 1 November 20X3 and 4 November 20X3 the following transactions took place:

1   Goods costing £38,400 were received from suppliers.

2   Goods that had cost £14,800 were sold for £20,000.

3   A customer returned, in good condition, some goods which had been sold to him in October for £600 and which had cost £400.

4   The company returned goods that had cost £1,800 in October to the supplier, and received a credit note for them.

What figure should appear in the company's financial statements at 31 October 20X3 for closing inventory, based on this information?

A   £458,700

B   £505,900

C   £508,700

D   £461,500

LO 3c

15  In preparing its financial statements for the current year, a company's closing inventory was understated by £300,000.

What will be the effect of this error if it remains uncorrected?

A   The current year's profit will be overstated and next year's profit will be understated

B   The current year's profit will be understated but there will be no effect on next year's profit

C   The current year's profit will be understated and next year's profit will be overstated

D   The current year's profit will be overstated but there will be no effect on next year's profit

LO 2a

16  At 30 September 20X3 the closing inventory of a company amounted to £386,400.

The following items were included in this total at cost:

1  1,000 items which had cost £18 each. These items were all sold in October 20X3 for £15 each, with selling expenses of £800.

2  Five items which had been in inventory for many years and which had been purchased for £100 each, sold in October 20X3 for £1,000 each, net of selling expenses.

What figure should appear in the company's statement of financial position at 30 September 20X3 for inventory?

A  £382,600

B  £390,200

C  £368,400

D  £400,600

LO 3c

17  The inventory value for the financial statements of Q for the year ended 31 December 20X4 was based on an inventory count on 4 January 20X5, which gave a total inventory value of £836,200.

Between 31 December 20X4 and 4 January 20X5, the following transactions took place:

|  | £ |
| --- | --- |
| Purchases of goods | 8,600 |
| Sales of goods (profit margin 30% on sales) | 14,000 |
| Goods returned by Q to supplier | 700 |

What adjusted figure should be included in the financial statements for inventories at 31 December 20X4?

A  £838,100

B  £842,300

C  £818,500

D  £834,300

LO 3c

18  The closing inventory of Epsilon amounted to £284,000 at cost at 30 September 20X1, the date of the statement of financial position. This total includes the following two inventory lines.

   1   500 items which had cost £15 each and which were included at £7,500. These items were found to have been defective at the date of the statement of financial position. Remedial work after that date cost £1,800 and they were then sold shortly afterwards for £20 each. Selling expenses were £400.

   2   100 items which had cost £10 each. After the date of the statement of financial position they were sold for £8 each, with selling expenses of £150.

The figure which should appear in Epsilon's statement of financial position for inventory is

A   £283,650

B   £284,350

C   £284,650

D   £291,725

LO 3c

19  Lamp makes the following purchases in the year ending 31 December 20X9.

|       |           | Units | £/unit | Total(£) |
|-------|-----------|-------|--------|----------|
| (i)   | 21.01.X9  | 100   | 12.00  | 1,200    |
| (ii)  | 30.04.X9  | 300   | 12.50  | 3,750    |
| (iii) | 31.07.X9  | 40    | 12.80  | 512      |
| (iv)  | 01.09.X9  | 60    | 13.00  | 780      |
| (v)   | 11.11.X9  | 80    | 13.50  | 1,080    |

At the year end 200 units are in inventory but 8 are damaged and are only worth £10 per unit. These are identified as having been part of the 11.11.X9 delivery. Lamp operates a FIFO system for valuing inventory.

The figure for inventories at 31.12.X9 is

A   £2,450

B   £2,525

C   £2,594

D   £2,700

LO 1c

20 Bouncy Balls plc has 40 units of its special spongy balls in inventory as at 30 November 20X7. The product costs £5 per unit to manufacture and can be sold for £15 per unit. Half of the units in inventory at the year end have been damaged and will require rectification work costing £10 per unit before they can be sold. Selling costs are £1 per unit.

The value of inventory at 30 November 20X7 is

A    £160

B    £180

C    £200

D    £600

LO 1c

21 The closing inventory of Stacks plc amounted to £58,200 *excluding* the following two inventory lines:

(i)    200 items which had cost £15 each. These items were found to be defective at the date of the statement of financial position. Rectification work after that date amounted to £1,200 for the batch, after which they were sold for £17.50 each, with selling expenses totalling £300 for the batch.

(ii)   400 items which had cost £2 each. All were sold after the date of the statement of financial position for £1.50 each, with selling expenses of £200 for the batch.

Which figure should appear in the statement of financial position of Stacks plc for inventory?

A    £62,000

B    £61,600

C    £60,600

D    £61,000

LO 3c

22 Fenton plc is a manufacturer of PCs. The company makes two different models, the M1 and M2, and has 100 of each in inventory at the year end.

Costs and related data for a unit of each model are as follows:

|                                      | M1 | M2 |
|--------------------------------------|----|----|
|                                      | £  | £  |
| Costs to date                        | 230 | 350 |
| Selling price                        | 400 | 500 |
| Modification costs to enable sale    | 110 | – |
| Delivery costs                       | 65 | 75 |

The figure for inventory that should appear in the statement of financial position at the year end is

A    £57,500

B    £58,000

C    £65,000

D    £65,500

LO 3c

23 When valuing inventory at cost, which of the following shows the correct method of arriving at cost?

| | Include inward transport costs | Include production overheads |
|---|---|---|
| A | Yes | No |
| B | No | Yes |
| C | Yes | Yes |
| D | No | No |

LO 1c

24 A trader who fixes her selling prices by adding 50% to cost actually achieved a mark-up of 45%.

Which of the following factors could account for the shortfall?

A Sales were lower than expected.

B The value of the opening inventories had been overstated.

C The closing inventories of the business were higher than the opening inventories.

D Goods taken from inventories by the proprietor were recorded by debiting drawings and crediting purchases with the cost of the goods.

LO 2a

25 Cornucopia plc has a standard mark-up of 25% on cost. During 20X9, its sales were £125,000 and its purchases were £80,000. Opening inventory was £35,000. The company did not carry out an inventory count at 31.12.X9 and has no records of an inventory figure at that date.

Using the information above the closing inventory should be

A £15,000

B £21,250

C £48,750

D £55,000

LO 1c

26 The gross profit margin is 20% where

A Cost of sales is £100,000 and sales are £120,000

B Cost of sales is £100,000 and sales are £125,000

C Cost of sales is £80,000 and gross profit is £16,000

D Cost of sales is £80,000 and sales are £96,000

LO 2a

27 Which of the following factors could cause a company's gross profit margin to fall below the expected level?

A    Overstatement of closing inventories.

B    The incorrect inclusion in purchases of invoices relating to goods supplied in the following period.

C    The inclusion in sales of the proceeds of sale of non-current assets.

D    Increased cost of carriage charges borne by the company on goods sent to customers.

LO 1c

28 An extract from a business's income statement is as follows:

|  | £ | £ |
|---|---|---|
| Revenue | | 115,200 |
| Opening inventory | 21,000 | |
| Purchases | 80,000 | |
| Closing inventory | (5,000) | |
| | | (96,000) |
| | | 19,200 |

The mark-up achieved is

A    14.8%

B    16.7%

C    20.0%

D    83.3%

LO 1c

29 An extended trial balance is being drawn up and closing inventory of £13,600 is to be entered in the adjustments columns and then extended into the income statement and statement of financial position columns.

Which income statement column would the figure for closing inventory be entered into?

A    Debit

B    Credit

Which statement of financial position column would the figure for closing inventory be entered into?

C    Debit

D    Credit

LO 1c

30  Quince plc's initial trial balance as at 31 May 20X3 has already been entered on the extended trial balance for the 12 month reporting period.

*Extended trial balance (extract)*

|  | Trial balance £ | £ |
|---|---|---|
| Opening inventory (at 1 June 20X2) | 456,875 | |
| Closing inventory (at 31 May 20X3) | | |

Inventory was counted on 31 May 20X3 and its cost has been established at £572,904.  Of this, inventory costing £27,485 is damaged and is estimated to have a net realisable value of only £15,000.  In the adjustments columns on the extended trial balance Quince plc should make TWO entries:

A  Debit £456,875 to the opening inventory account

B  Debit £545,419 to the closing inventory account

C  Debit £560,419 to the closing inventory account

D  Debit £572,904 to the closing inventory account

E  Credit £456,875 to the opening inventory account

F  Credit £545,419 to the closing inventory account

G  Credit £560,419 to the closing inventory account

H  Credit £572,904 to the closing inventory account

LO 1c

---

31  Franz plc is a manufacturer. Its 12 month reporting period ends on 31 July and it adopts the average cost (AVCO) method of inventory usage and valuation. At 1 August 20X4 it held inventory of 2,400 units of the material Zobdo, valued at £10.00 each. In the year to 31 July 20X5 there were the following inventory movements of Zobdo:

| 14 November 20X4 | Sell | 900 units |
| 28 January 20X5 | Purchase | 1,200 units for £20,100 |
| 7 May 20X5 | Sell | 1,800 units |

What was the value of Franz plc's closing inventory of Zobdo at 31 July 20X5?

A  £11,700

B  £9,000

C  £15,075

D  £35,100

LO 1c

---

32  For many years Wrigley plc has experienced rising prices for raw material X, and has kept constant inventory levels. It has always used the AVCO inventory valuation method. If Wrigley plc had always used the FIFO valuation method, in each successive year's financial statements this would result in

A  Lower cost of sales and higher closing inventory value

B  Lower cost of sales and lower closing inventory value

C  Higher cost of sales and lower closing inventory value

D  Higher cost of sales and higher closing inventory value

LO 1c, 3a

33  During the year ended 31 March 20X4 Boogie plc suffered a major fire at its factory, in which inventory that had cost £36,000 was destroyed. An insurance payment of 80% of the cost has been agreed but not received at the year end.

To take account of these matters on its extended trial balance Boogie plc should debit trade and other receivables with £28,800 and:

A   Debit Administrative expenses £36,000, Credit Purchases £28,800, Credit Revenue £36,000

B   Debit Administrative expenses £7,200, Credit Purchases £36,000

C   Debit Administrative expenses £36,000, Credit Purchases £36,000, Credit Other income £28,800

D   Debit Administrative expenses £7,200, Credit Inventory £36,000

LO 2a, 2d

1     Cataract plc purchases a machine for which the supplier's list price is £28,000. Cataract plc pays £23,000 in cash and trades in an old machine, which has a carrying amount of £8,000. It is the company's policy to depreciate machines at the rate of 10% per annum on cost.

      What is the carrying amount of the machine after one year?

      A     £18,000

      B     £25,200

      C     £20,700

      D     £22,200

                                                     LO 1c

2     Demolition plc purchases a machine for £15,000 on 1 January 20X1. After incurring transportation costs of £1,300 and spending £2,500 on installing the machine it breaks down and costs £600 to repair. Depreciation is charged at 10% per annum.

      At what carrying amount will the machine be shown in Demolition plc's statement of financial position at 31 December 20X1?

      A     £13,500

      B     £14,670

      C     £16,920

      D     £18,800

                                                     LO 3c

3     A company buys a machine on 31 August 20X0 for £22,000. It has an expected life of seven years and an estimated residual value of £1,000. On 30 June 20X4 the machine is sold for £9,000. The company's year end is 31 December. Its accounting policy is to charge depreciation monthly using the straight line method.

      The loss on disposal of the machine which will appear in the income statement for the year ended 31 December 20X4 is

      A     £1,000

      B     £1,500

      C     £3,500

      D     £5,800

                                                      LO 3c

4   Derek plc purchased a van on 1 October 20X0 for a total cost of £22,000 by paying £17,500 cash and trading in an old van. The old van had cost £20,000 and the related accumulated depreciation was £14,200.

The loss on disposal in Derek plc's income statement for the year ended 31 December 20X0 is

A   £1,300

B   £2,000

C   £2,500

D   £5,800

LO 3c

5   Vernon plc purchased some new equipment on 1 April 20X1 for £6,000. The scrap value of the new equipment in 5 years' time is estimated to be £300. Vernon charges depreciation monthly on the straight line basis.

What is the depreciation charge for the equipment in Vernon plc's reporting period of twelve months to 30 September 20X1?

A   £570

B   £1,140

C   £600

D   £1,200

LO 3c

6   A car has a list price of £23,500 but the garage gives Ride plc a 10% trade discount. In settlement the garage accepts a cheque for £18,000, together with an old company car. The amount to be capitalised by Ride plc for the new car is:

A   £16,200

B   £18,000

C   £21,150

D   £23,500

LO 1c

7  A company purchased a car for £18,000 on 1 January 20X0.

   The car was traded in on 1 January 20X2. The new car has a list price of £30,000 and the garage offered a part-exchange allowance of £5,000.

   The company provides depreciation on cars using the reducing balance method at a rate of 25% per annum.

   What loss on disposal will be recognised in the income statement for the year ended 31 December 20X2?

   A   £5,125

   B   £8,500

   C   £10,125

   D   £11,175

   LO 3c

---

8  What is the reasoning behind charging depreciation in historical cost accounting?

   A   To ensure funds are available for the eventual replacement of the asset.

   B   To comply with the consistency concept.

   C   To ensure the asset is included in the statement of financial position at the lower of cost and net realisable value.

   D   To match the cost of the non-current asset with the revenue that the asset generates.

   LO 1c

---

9  Which of the following is excluded from the cost of a tangible non-current asset?

   A   Site preparation costs

   B   Legal fees

   C   Costs of a design error

   D   Installation costs

   LO 1c

---

10  Which of the following statements about intangible assets in public company financial statements are correct?

   1   Internally generated goodwill should not be capitalised.

   2   Purchased goodwill should normally be amortised through the income statement.

   3   Development expenditure must be capitalised if certain conditions are met.

   A   1 and 3 only

   B   1 and 2 only

   C   2 and 3 only

   D   1, 2 and 3

   LO 1c, 3c

11 Your firm bought a machine for £5,000 on 1 January 20X1, when it had an expected useful life of four years and an expected residual value of £1,000. Straight-line depreciation is to be applied on a monthly basis. On 31 December 20X3, the machine was sold for £1,600.

The amount to be entered in the 20X3 income statement for profit or loss on disposal is

A    profit of £600

B    loss of £600

C    profit of £350

D    loss of £400

LO 3c

12 An asset was purchased by Prance plc on 1 January 20X1 for:

|                    | £         |
|--------------------|-----------|
| Cost               | 1,000,000 |
| Annual licence fee | 15,000    |
| Total              | 1,015,000 |

The business adopts a date of 31 December as its reporting year end.

The asset was traded in for a replacement asset on 1 January 20X4 at an agreed value of £500,000.

It has been depreciated at 25% per annum on the reducing-balance method.

What figure is included regarding this disposal in the income statement for the year ended December 20X4?

A    £25,000 profit

B    £78,125 profit

C    £62,500 loss

D    £250,000 loss

LO 3c

13 An asset register showed a total carrying amount of £67,460. A non-current asset costing £15,000 had been sold for £4,000, making a loss on disposal of £1,250. No entries had been made in the asset register for this disposal.

The correct balance on the asset register is

A    £42,710

B    £51,210

C    £53,710

D    £62,210

LO 2b

14 An organisation's asset register shows a total carrying amount of £145,600. The non-current asset accounts in the nominal ledger show a carrying amount of £135,600. The difference is due to an asset having been disposed of but not having been eliminated from the asset register. This disposal could have taken place

    A    With disposal proceeds of £15,000 and a profit on disposal of £5,000

    B    With disposal proceeds of £15,000 and a carrying amount of £5,000

    C    With disposal proceeds of £15,000 and a loss on disposal of £5,000

    D    With disposal proceeds of £5,000 and a carrying amount of £5,000

LO 2b

15 On 1 January 20X5 a company purchased some plant.

The invoice showed

|  | £ |
|---|---|
| Cost of plant | 48,000 |
| Delivery to factory | 400 |
| One year warranty covering breakdown during 20X5 | 800 |
|  | 49,200 |

Modifications costing £2,200 were necessary to enable the plant to be installed.

What amount should be capitalised for the plant in the company's records?

    A    £51,400

    B    £48,000

    C    £50,600

    D    £48,400

LO 1c

16 A company's plant and machinery ledger account for the year ended 30 September 20X2 was as follows:

PLANT AND MACHINERY

| 20X1 | | £ | 20X2 | | £ |
|---|---|---|---|---|---|
| 1 Oct | Balance | 381,200 | 1 Jun | Disposal account – cost of asset sold | 36,000 |
| 1 Dec | Cash – addition at cost | 18,000 | 30 Sep | Balance | 363,200 |
| | | 399,200 | | | 399,200 |

The company's policy is to charge depreciation at 20% per year on the straight line basis.

What is the depreciation charge in the income statement for the year ended 30 September 20X2?

    A    £74,440

    B    £84,040

    C    £72,640

    D    £76,840

LO 1c, 3c

17 The carrying amount of a company's non-current assets was £200,000 at 1 August 20X0. During the year ended 31 July 20X1, the company sold non-current assets for £25,000 on which it made a loss of £5,000. The depreciation charge for the year was £20,000. The carrying amount of non-current assets at 31 July 20X1 is

A £150,000

B £175,000

C £180,000

D £195,000

LO 3c

---

18 A plant account is shown below:

PLANT

| 20X2 | | £ | 20X2 | | £ |
|---|---|---|---|---|---|
| 1 Jan | Balance (plant purchased 20X0) | 380,000 | 1 Oct | Disposal account – cost of plant sold | 30,000 |
| 1 Apr | Cash – plant purchased | 51,000 | 31 Dec | Balance | 401,000 |
| | | 431,000 | | | 431,000 |

The company's policy is to charge depreciation on plant monthly at 20% per year on the straight line basis.

What should the company's plant depreciation charge be in the income statement for the year ended 31 December 20X2?

A £82,150

B £79,150

C £77,050

D £74,050

LO 1c, 3c

19 A company's policy for depreciation of its plant and machinery is to charge depreciation monthly at 20% per year on cost. The company's plant and machinery account for the year ended 30 September 20X4 is shown below:

PLANT AND MACHINERY

| | £ | | | | £ |
|---|---|---|---|---|---|
| 20X3 | | | 20X4 | | |
| 1 Oct Balance (all plant purchased after 20X0) | 200,000 | | 30 Jun Disposal account | | 40,000 |
| | | | 30 Sep Balance | | 210,000 |
| 20X4 | | | | | |
| 1 Apr Cash purchase of plant | 50,000 | | | | |
| | 250,000 | | | | 250,000 |

What should be the depreciation charge in the income statement for plant and machinery (excluding any profit or loss on the disposal) for the year ended 30 September 20X4?

A £43,000

B £51,000

C £42,000

D £45,000

LO 1c, 3c

20 Beta plc purchased some plant and equipment on 1 July 20X1 for £40,000. The estimated scrap value of the plant in ten years' time is estimated to be £4,000. Beta plc's policy is to charge depreciation monthly on the straight line basis.

The depreciation charge on the plant in Beta's income statement for the reporting period of twelve months ending 30 September 20X1 should be

A £900

B £1,000

C £2,700

D £3,000

LO 1c, 3c

21 Exe plc, which has a year end of 31 December, purchased a machine on I January 20X1 for £35,000. It was depreciated at 40% per annum on the reducing balance basis. On I January 20X4 Exe plc part-exchanged this machine for a more advanced model. It paid £30,000 and realised a profit on disposal of £2,440.

The price of the new machine was

A £10,000

B £34,680

C £35,120

D £40,000

LO 1c

22  Automat plc purchases a machine for which the supplier's list price is £18,000. Automat plc pays £13,000 in cash and trades in an old machine which has a carrying amount of £8,000. It is the company's policy to depreciate such machines monthly at the rate of 10% per annum on cost.

The carrying amount of the new machine after one year is

A    £16,200

B    £18,000

C    £18,900

D    £21,000

LO 1c, 3c

23  Beehive plc bought a car on 1 January 20X7 for £10,000 and decided to depreciate it at 30% per annum on a reducing balance basis. It was disposed of on 1 January 20X9 for £6,000.

The net effect on the income statement for the year ended 31 December 20X9 is a credit of

A    £1,100

B    £3,000

C    £4,000

D    £5,100

LO 1c, 3c

24  Ben plc purchased a machine for £120,000 on 1 October 20X8. The estimated useful life is 4 years with a residual value of £4,000. Ben plc uses the straight line method for depreciation and charges depreciation on a monthly basis.

The charge for depreciation in the income statement for the year ended 31 December 20X8 is

A    £4,833

B    £7,250

C    £7,500

D    £29,000

LO 1c, 3c

25  Sam plc's income statement for the year ended 31 December 20X4 showed a net profit of £83,600. It was later found that £18,000 paid for the purchase of a van on 1 January 20X4 had been debited to motor expenses account. It is the company's policy to depreciate vans at 25% per year.

What is the net profit after adjusting for this error?

A    £106,100

B    £70,100

C    £97,100

D    £101,600

LO 2a

26 On 1 January 20X4 Joffa plc purchased a new machine at a cost of £96,720. Delivery costs were £3,660 and internal administration costs of £9,450 were incurred. At that time Joffa plc planned to replace the machine in 5 years, when it would have no value, and to depreciate the machine on a straight line basis.

Joffa plc decides on 1 January 20X6 that the machine only has one remaining year of useful life. There is no expected change to the residual value at the end of its life.

How much depreciation will be charged in respect of this machine in Joffa plc's income statement for the year ended 31 December 20X6?

A    £58,032

B    £60,228

C    £65,898

D    £33,460

LO 1c, 3c

27 The bookkeeper of Meridian plc has been attempting to reconcile its list of non-current assets held to the non-current assets accounts in the nominal ledger. The list of non-current assets shows a carrying amount of £300,070, but the net balance of the non-current assets cost and accumulated depreciation accounts in the nominal ledger shows a figure of £351,080. On investigation the bookkeeper has discovered the only error made during the year was that the disposal of one asset has not yet been recorded in the nominal ledger.

Which TWO of the following scenarios would, individually, explain this difference?

A    An asset was disposed of for £40,950 resulting in a profit on disposal of £10,060

B    An asset was disposed of for £40,950 resulting in a loss on disposal of £10,060

C    An asset was disposed of for £61,070 resulting in a profit on disposal of £10,060

D    An asset was disposed of for £61,070 resulting in a loss on disposal of £10,060

LO 2b

28 On 1 June 20X3 Spam plc purchased some plant at a price of £43,000. It cost £1,500 to transport the plant to Spam plc's premises and set it up, plus £900 for a licence to operate it. The plant had a useful life of 8 years and a residual value of £3,500. On 1 June 20X5 the directors of Spam plc decided to change the depreciation method to reducing balance, at 40%.

What is the carrying amount of Spam plc's machine in its statement of financial position at 31 May 20X6?

A    £20,025

B    £20,280

C    £20,550

D    £20,955

LO 3c

29  On 1 April 20X5 Herepath plc bought a Foxy car for £23,500. The company's depreciation policy for cars is 30% per annum using the reducing balance method. On 1 April 20X7 the Foxy was part exchanged for a Vizgo car, which had a purchase price of £28,200. Herepath plc handed over a cheque to the seller for £19,350, in final settlement.

What was Herepath plc's profit or loss on the disposal of the Foxy?

A  £5,150 loss

B  £7,835 profit

C  £2,665 loss

D  £6,250 loss

LO 1c

30  Muncher plc includes profits and losses on disposal of non-current assets in administrative expenses in its income statement.  Depreciation is charged on fixtures and fittings at 20% using the reducing balance method.  On 1 July 20X6 some fixtures that cost £4,000 on 1 July 20X3 were sold for £150.  In the administrative expenses account Muncher plc must:

A  Debit £1,450

B  Credit £1,450

C  Debit £1,898

D  Credit £1,898

LO 1c

31  Redruth plc commenced trading on 1 April 20X3.  The carrying amount of plant and equipment in Redruth plc's financial statements as at 31 March 20X5 was £399,960.  The cost of these assets was £614,500.  On 31 March 20X6 an asset costing £11,500 was acquired.  Depreciation is charged on plant and equipment monthly at an annual rate of 25% straight line.  There are no residual values.

The carrying amount of Redruth plc's plant and equipment in its statement of financial position at 31 March 20X6 is:

A  £254,960

B  £257,835

C  £299,970

D  £308,595

LO 3c

32  McClown plc has the following information in its financial statements relating to fixtures and fittings as at 31 December:

|  | 20X9 £ | 20X8 £ |
|---|---|---|
| Cost | 600,000 | 480,000 |
| Accumulated depreciation | 180,000 | 218,000 |
| Carrying amount | 420,000 | 262,000 |

During the year to 31 December 20X9, the following transactions occurred in relation to fixtures and fittings:

Additions £284,000

Sales proceeds from disposals £178,800

Depreciation charge £66,400

What is McClown plc's profit or loss on disposals of fixtures and fittings in the year ended 31 December 20X9?

A  £119,200 loss

B  £119,200 profit

C  £196,800 profit

D  £196,800 loss

LO 1c

33  Morse plc has the following note to its statement of financial position relating to plant and machinery as at 31 May.

|  | 20X7 £ | 20X6 £ |
|---|---|---|
| Cost | 110,000 | 92,000 |
| Accumulated depreciation | 72,000 | 51,000 |
| Carrying amount | 38,000 | 41,000 |

During the year to 31 May 20X7, the following transactions occurred in relation to plant and machinery:

Additions £39,000

Loss on disposals £2,000

Depreciation charge £27,000

What were the proceeds from disposals of plant and machinery received by Morse plc in the year to 31 May 20X7?

A  £7,000

B  £8,000

C  £13,000

D  £17,000

LO 1c, 3a

34  Anaconda plc acquired a machine on 31 March 20X4, its year end, for £196,600. It gave the seller a cheque for £110,000 and handed over an old machine with a carrying amount at that date of £34,400. This machine had cost £60,000. A further sum of £42,000 was then due to the supplier of the machine as the final payment.

The only entries made before the initial trial balance was drawn up were to credit cash £110,000 and credit other payables £42,000.

As well as crediting Suspense with £152,000, which of the following sets of adjustments should be made on the extended trial balance to reflect the purchase and disposal in Anaconda plc's financial statements?

A  Debit Machine – cost £196,600, Debit Machine – accumulated depreciation £34,400, Credit Disposal £79,000

B  Debit Machine – cost £136,600, Debit Machine – accumulated depreciation £34,400, Credit Disposal £19,000

C  Debit Machine – cost £196,600, Debit Machine – accumulated depreciation £25,600, Credit Disposal £70,200

D  Debit Machine – cost £136,600, Debit Machine – accumulated depreciation £25,600, Credit Disposal £10,200

LO 2b, 2d

35  Gilbert plc acquired a new truck on 1 July 20X4 for £99,900 including VAT at 20%. The company depreciates all vehicles straight line at 20% per annum on a monthly basis.

What is the carrying amount of Gilbert plc's truck at 31 December 20X4?

A  £89,910

B  £83,250

C  £66,600

D  £74,925

LO 3c

36  Crocker plc, a retailer, depreciates all vehicles monthly over five years. On 31 October 20X9 Crocker plc bought a car at a cost of £17,625 plus VAT, trading in an old car that had cost £16,800 including VAT on 1 July 20X7. A cheque for £13,500 was also handed over. VAT is at a rate of 20%.

In respect of this disposal in its income statement for the year ended 31 December 20X9 Crocker plc will show a loss of:

A  £2,430

B  £4,835

C  £5,955

D  £1,310

LO 1c, 3c

37 Plummet plc is preparing its income statement for the year ended 31 December 20X4. On the initial trial balance at that date administrative expenses have a debit balance of £684,000 before accounting for depreciation and profits/losses on disposal in respect of the company's computer equipment. At 31 December 20X3 Plummet plc had computer equipment that cost £1,004,408, all of which had been purchased on 1 January 20X2, and it had accumulated depreciation of £697,600. A computer system costing £6,800 was sold on 1 January 20X4 for £1,800. Computer equipment is depreciated monthly over four years.

The amount to be disclosed as administrative expenses in Plummet plc's income statement for the year ended 31 December 20X4 is:

A £933,402

B £935,002

C £936,702

D £963,702

LO 1c 3c

38 Dukakis plc had computer equipment with a carrying amount at 1 April 20X2 of £150,000. On that date it traded in a computer which had cost £24,000 on 1 April 20X0 for a new computer which cost £34,600, handing over a cheque in full settlement for £18,000. Dukakis plc depreciates computers at 40% per annum on the reducing balance.

How much depreciation will be charged in Dukakis plc's income statement for the year ended 31 March 20X3 in respect of computers?

A £66,640

B £73,840

C £56,544

D £70,384

LO 1c, 3c

1   A company's share capital consists of 20,000 25p equity shares all of which were issued at a premium of 20%. The market value of the shares is currently 70p each.

What is the balance on the company's equity share capital account?

A   £5,000

B   £6,000

C   £14,000

D   £24,000

LO 1c, 1d

2   Which of the following may appear as current liabilities in a company's statement of financial position?

1   Loan due for repayment within 1 year

2   Taxation

3   Warranty provision

A   1, 2 and 3

B   1 and 2 only

C   1 and 3 only

D   2 and 3 only

LO 3c

3   At 30 June 20X5 Meredith plc had the following balances:

|  | £m |
|---|---|
| Equity shares of £1 each | 100 |
| Share premium account | 80 |

During the year ended 30 June 20X6, the following transactions took place:

1 September 20X5: A 1 for 2 bonus issue of equity shares, using the share premium account.

1 January 20X6: A 2 for 5 rights issue at £1.50 per share, taken up fully paid.

What are the balances on each account at 30 June 20X6?

|  | Share capital (£m) | Share premium account (£m) |
|---|---|---|
| A | 210 | 110 |
| B | 210 | 60 |
| C | 240 | 30 |
| D | 240 | 80 |

LO 1c, 1d, 3c

4    Klaxon plc made an issue of shares for cash of 1,000,000 50p shares at a premium of 30p per share.

Which of the following journals correctly records the issue?

A    Debit Share capital £500,000, Debit Share premium £300,000, Credit Cash at bank £800,000

B    Debit Cash at bank £800,000, Credit Share capital £500,000, Credit Share premium £300,000

C    Debit Cash at bank £1,300,000, Credit Share capital £1,000,000, Credit Share premium £300,000

D    Debit Share capital £1,000,000, Debit Share premium £300,000, Credit Cash at bank £1,300,000

LO 1c, 1d, 2d

---

5    Sanders plc issued 50,000 equity shares of 25p each at a premium of 50p per share. The cash received was correctly recorded but the full amount was credited to the equity share capital account.

Which of the following journals corrects this error?

A    Debit Share premium £25,000, Credit Share capital £25,000

B    Debit Share capital £25,000, Credit Share premium £25,000

C    Debit Share capital £37,500, Credit Share premium £37,500

D    Debit Share capital £25,000, Credit Cash at bank £25,000

LO 1c, 1d, 2d

---

6    Which of the following journals correctly records a bonus issue of shares?

A    Debit Cash at bank, Credit Share capital

B    Debit Share capital, Credit Share premium

C    Debit Share premium, Credit Share capital

D    Debit Investments, Credit Cash at bank

LO 1d, 2d

---

7    At 31 December 20X1 the capital structure of a company was as follows:

|  | £ |
|---|---|
| 100,000 equity shares of 50p each | 50,000 |
| Share premium account | 180,000 |

During 20X2 the company made a 1 for 2 bonus issue, using the share premium account for the purpose, and later issued for cash another 60,000 shares at 80p per share.

What is the company's capital structure at 31 December 20X2?

|  | Equity share capital | Share premium account |
|---|---|---|
| A | £130,000 | £173,000 |
| B | £105,000 | £173,000 |
| C | £130,000 | £137,000 |
| D | £105,000 | £137,000 |

LO 1c, 1d

8    Evon plc issued 1,000,000 equity shares of 25p each at a price of £1.10 per share, all received in cash.

Which of the following journals records this issue?

A    Debit Cash at bank £1,100,000, Credit Share capital £250,000, Credit Share premium £850,000

B    Debit Share capital £250,000, Debit Share premium £850,000, Credit Cash at bank £1,100,000

C    Debit Cash at bank £1,100,000, Credit Share capital £1,100,000

D    Debit Cash at bank £1,100,000, Credit Share capital £250,000, Credit Retained earnings £850,000

LO 1c, 1d, 2d

---

9    A material profit or loss on the sale of part of the entity must appear in the income statement as an extraordinary item.

A    True

B    False

Drawings should be included in the income statement.

C    True

D    False

LO 3c

---

10   At 30 June 20X2 Brandon plc's capital structure was as follows:

|  | £ |
|---|---|
| 500,000 equity shares of 25p each | 125,000 |
| Share premium account | 100,000 |

In the year ended 30 June 20X3 the company made a 1 for 2 rights issue at £1 per share and this was taken up in full. Later in the year the company made a 1 for 5 bonus issue, using the share premium account for the purpose.

What was the company's capital structure at 30 June 20X3?

|  | Equity share capital | Share premium account |
|---|---|---|
| A | £450,000 | £25,000 |
| B | £225,000 | £250,000 |
| C | £225,000 | £325,000 |
| D | £212,500 | £262,500 |

LO 1c, 3c

11   At 1 July 20X4 Xando plc's capital structure was as follows:

|                                              | £       |
|----------------------------------------------|---------|
| Share capital 1,000,000 shares of 50p each   | 500,000 |
| Share premium account                        | 400,000 |

In the year ended 30 June 20X5 Xando plc made the following share issues:

1 January 20X5:

A 1 for 4 bonus issue.

1 April 20X5:

A 1 for 10 rights issue at £1.50 per share.

What will be the balances on the company's share capital and share premium accounts at 30 June 20X5 as a result of these issues?

|   | Share capital | Share premium account |
|---|---------------|-----------------------|
| A | £687,500      | £650,000              |
| B | £675,000      | £375,000              |
| C | £687,500      | £150,000              |
| D | £687,500      | £400,000              |

LO 1c, 3c

12   A company has the following capital structure:

|                          | £      |
|--------------------------|--------|
| 200,000 shares of 25p    | 50,000 |
| Share premium account    | 75,000 |

It makes a 1 for 5 rights issue at £1.25, which is fully subscribed.

The balance on the share premium account following the rights issue is

A   £35,000

B   £75,000

C   £85,000

D   £115,000

LO 1c, 3c

13   At 1 April 20X8 the share capital and share premium account of a company were as follows:

|                                                      | £       |
|------------------------------------------------------|---------|
| Share capital – 300,000 equity shares of 25p each    | 75,000  |
| Share premium account                                | 200,000 |

During the year ended 31 March 20X9 the following events took place:

1    On 1 October 20X8 the company made a 1 for 5 rights issue at £1.20 per share.

2    On 1 January 20X9 the company made a 1 for 3 bonus issue using the share premium account to do so.

The correct balance on the share capital account at 31 March 20X9 is

A    £90,000

B    £120,000

C    £360,000

D    £480,000

LO 1c, 3c

**The following information is relevant for questions 14 and 15**

When Q plc's trial balance failed to agree, a suspense account was opened for the difference. The trial balance totals were:

|        | £       |
|--------|---------|
| Debit  | 864,390 |
| Credit | 860,930 |

The company does not have control accounts for its receivables and payables ledgers.

14   Which of the following errors can be corrected **without** affecting the suspense account?

A    In recording an issue of shares at par, cash received of £333,000 was credited to the equity share capital account as £330,000.

B    Cash £2,800 paid for plant repairs was correctly accounted for in the cash book but was credited to the plant asset account.

C    A cheque for £78,400 paid for the purchase of a car was debited to the motor vehicles account as £87,400.

D    A contra between the receivables ledger and the payables ledger for £1,200 was debited in the receivables ledger and credited in the payables ledger.

LO 2a, 2b

15   What will the balance on Q plc's suspense account be after making the necessary entries to correct the errors affecting the suspense account?

A    £2,940 Debit

B    £15,060 Credit

C    £14,140 Debit

D    £9,860 Debit

LO 2a, 2b

16 Which of the following journal entries may be accepted as being correct according to their narratives?

|   |   | DR £ | CR £ |
|---|---|---|---|
| A | Wages account | 38,000 | |
| | Purchases account | 49,000 | |
| | Buildings account | | 87,000 |
| | *Labour and materials used in construction of extension to factory* | | |
| B | Directors' personal accounts  A | 30,000 | |
| | B | 40,000 | |
| | Directors' remuneration | | 70,000 |
| | *Directors' bonuses transferred to their accounts* | | |
| C | Suspense account | 10,000 | |
| | Sales account | | 10,000 |
| | *Correction of £10,000 undercast of sales account* | | |
| D | Discount received account | 2,000 | |
| | Suspense account | | 2,000 |
| | *Correction of misposting of discount received from cash book* | | |

LO 1c, 2d

17 At 30 June 20X2 a company had £1m 8% loan notes in issue, interest being paid half-yearly on 30 June and 31 December.

On 30 September 20X2 the company redeemed £250,000 of these loan notes at par, paying interest due to that date.

On 1 April 20X3 the company issued £500,000 7% loan notes at par, interest payable half-yearly on 31 March and 30 September.

What figure should appear in the company's income statement for finance costs in the year ended 30 June 20X3?

A £88,750

B £82,500

C £65,000

D £73,750

LO 3c

18 A company has a balance of £3,200 (debit) on its tax account at 31 December 20X7 relating to the tax payable on the 20X6 profits. The company's estimated tax liability for the year to 31 December 20X7 is £24,500.

The tax charge in the income statement for the year ended 31 December 20X7 is

A £21,300

B £24,500

C £27,700

D £30,900

LO 3c

19  A company is preparing its financial statements for the year ending 31 March 20X7. The initial trial
    balance has the following figures relating to tax:

    |                                                 | £      |
    |-------------------------------------------------|--------|
    | Tax payable at 1 April 20X6                     | 14,300 |
    | Tax paid during the year ended 31 March 20X7    | 12,700 |

    The estimated tax liability for the year ended 31 March 20X7 is £15,600.

    The figure for tax expense in the company's income statement will be

    A    £12,700

    B    £14,000

    C    £17,200

    D    £28,300

    LO 3c

20  Which of the following accounting treatments derive from the accounting concept of accruals?

    (1)   Write down of a non-current asset which has suffered a fall in value

    (2)   Opening and closing inventory adjustments

    (3)   Capitalisation and amortisation of development expenditure

    A    (1) and (2)

    B    (3) only

    C    (2) and (3)

    D    (1) only

    LO 3b

21  Which of the following statements, if any, are correct?

    1    All non-current assets must be depreciated.

    2    In a company's published statement of financial position, tangible assets and intangible assets
         must be shown separately.

    A    1 only

    B    2 only

    C    Both 1 and 2

    D    Neither 1 nor 2

    LO 1c, 3c

22  Camelia plc is preparing its financial statements for the year ended 30 June 20X9. Its initial trial balance shows the following balances:

|  | £ |
|---|---|
| Accruals at 1 July 20X8 | 948 |
| Distribution costs paid | 130,647 |

Of the accruals at 1 July 20X8, £586 related to distribution costs. At 30 June 20X9 the equivalent figure is £654 for distribution costs.

In Camelia plc's income statement distribution costs will be:

A   £129,407

B   £130,579

C   £130,715

D   £131,887

LO 1c, 3c

---

23  On 1 January 20X6 Pigeon plc has £300,000 of 50p equity shares in issue, and a balance on share premium of £750,000. On 1 April 20X6 the company makes a 1 for 3 bonus issue.

The balance on Pigeon plc's share premium account at 31 December 20X6 is:

A   £450,000

B   £550,000

C   £650,000

D   £850,000

LO 1c, 1d

---

24  At 1 July 20X7 Leak plc owed £524,925 to suppliers plus £9,653 to staff in respect of bonuses. In the year to 30 June 20X8 it paid trade suppliers £1,249,506, and £34,682 in staff bonuses. Leak plc also posted £1,987,345 to its trade payables control account from the purchases day book, and received discounts of £12,824. At the end of the period it processed a contra with the receivables ledger of £8,236, and calculated that it owed staff bonuses of £12,762.

In its statement of financial position as at 30 June 20X8 Leak plc will have a figure for trade and other payables of:

A   £1,267,352

B   £1,241,704

C   £1,258,176

D   £1,283,824

LO 3c

25  Sham plc's income statement for the year to 31 January 20X7 shows tax expense of £42,560. In its statement of financial position at that date tax payable is £23,820. During the year Sham plc paid HMRC £40,000 in respect of tax for the year ended 31 January 20X6, but subsequently received a refund from HMRC for £2,680.

At 31 January 20X6 Sham plc's tax payable balance in its statement of financial position was

A  £23,940

B  £18,580

C  £23,700

D  £29,060

LO 1c, 3c

26  Monksford plc is preparing its financial statements for the year ended 31 December 20X1. Its initial trial balance shows the following balances:

|  | £ |
| --- | --- |
| Tax payable at 1 January 20X1 | 2,091 |
| Tax paid regarding 20X0 in 20X1 (as finally agreed with HMRC) | 1,762 |

The estimated tax due for the year ended 31 December 20X1 is £2,584. In Monksford plc's income statement for the year ended 31 December 20X1 the figure for tax expense will be:

A  £1,269

B  £2,255

C  £2,584

D  £2,913

LO 1c, 3c

27  Zenia plc is preparing its financial statements for the 12 month reporting period ended 31 August 20X6, having prepared an initial trial balance which includes the following balances:

|  | £ |
| --- | --- |
| Accruals at 1 September 20X5 | 948 |
| Interest paid | 2,733 |

Of the accruals at 1 September 20X5, £362 related to interest payable. At 31 August 20X6 accruals will include £419 related to interest payable.

In Zenia plc's income statement for the 12 month reporting period ended 31 August 20X6 the finance costs will be:

A  £2,204

B  £2,676

C  £2,733

D  £2,790

LO 1c, 3c

28 Wonka plc has the following ledger account balances as at 1 September 20X5:

Share capital (£0.50 equity shares) £200,000

Share premium £20,000

Retained earnings £793,442

On 1 November 20X5 Wonka plc made a 1 for 4 rights issue at £4.50 per share. On 31 August 20X6 it made a 2 for 1 bonus issue. Profit for the year to 31 August 20X6 was £100,000.

What are the balances on the three ledger accounts as at 31 August 20X6?

A   Share capital £1,500,000, Share premium £Nil, Retained earnings £813,442

B   Share capital £750,000, Share premium £Nil, Retained earnings £813,442

C   Share capital £750,000, Share premium £420,000, Retained earnings £393,442

D   Share capital £1,500,000, Share premium £Nil, Retained earnings £393,442

LO 1c, 1d

29 Grease plc is a large company with a share capital of 3 million 20p equity shares. To raise funds it has made a 1 for 4 rights issue of its equity shares at £3.60 per share. The rights issue was fully taken up but only £1.9 million had been paid up at the year end, 30 September 20X2. The only entry has been to debit cash at bank with £1.9 million.

On its extended trial balance Grease plc should:

A   Debit Other receivables £2,700,000, Credit Share capital £150,000, Credit Share premium £2,550,000

B   Debit Suspense £1,900,000, Debit Other receivables £800,000, Credit Share capital £750,000, Credit Share premium £1,950,000

C   Debit Other receivables £800,000, Credit Share capital £150,000, Credit Share premium £650,000

D   Debit Suspense £1,900,000, Debit Other receivables £800,000, Credit Share capital £150,000, Credit Share premium £2,550,000

LO 1d, 2d

30 In relation to purchases Lake plc records £9,801 in its purchases day book and £107 in its cash book in the year ended 31 January 20X4. The company's purchases accruals need to be £75 less than at the previous year end, and prepayments need to be £60 less.

What is the figure for purchases included in cost of sales in Lake plc's income statement for the year ended 31 January 20X4?

A   £9,893

B   £9,923

C   £9,786

D   £9,908

LO 1c, 3c

31 Wombat plc is a retailer that owns no properties and only has fixtures and fittings, purchased within the last six months, as non-current assets. The company has been experiencing trading problems for some time. The directors have concluded that the company is no longer a going concern and have changed the basis of preparing the financial statements to the break-up basis.

Which TWO of the following will be the immediate effects of changing to the break-up basis?

A    All fixtures and fittings are transferred from non-current to current assets

B    Fixtures and fittings are valued at their resale value

C    The company ceases to trade

D    A liquidator is appointed

LO 3b

32 Drange plc has share capital of 300,000 £1 shares at 1 March 20X7. These were issued at £1.50 per share. On 28 February 20X8 Drange plc made a 2 for 3 bonus issue. Before accounting for this the balance on the retained earnings reserve at 28 February 20X8 was £717,000.

In its statement of financial position at 28 February 20X8 the balance on Drange plc's retained earnings reserve will be

A    £517,000

B    £567,000

C    £667,000

D    £717,000

LO 1c, 1d, 3c

33 The trial balance of Albion plc, a manufacturer, as at the year end 30 April 20X4 included the following items:

1    Depreciation of delivery vehicles

2    Carriage inwards

(a)  In the income statement depreciation of delivery vehicles should be included in the heading

A    Cost of sales

B    Administrative expenses

C    Distribution costs

(b)  In the income statement carriage inwards from suppliers should be included in the heading

D    Cost of sales

E    Administrative expenses

F    Distribution costs

LO 3c

34  Rembrandt plc is finalising certain figures that will appear in its financial statements as at 30 September 20X7. In its initial trial balance at that date Rembrandt plc has a figure for tax payable as at 1 October 20X6 of £114,520. The total tax charge in the income statement for the year to 30 September 20X7 is £145,670, and tax paid in the year was £123,090.

The tax payable balance that will appear in Rembrandt plc's statement of financial position as at 30 September 20X7 is

A    £91,940

B    £114,520

C    £137,100

D    £382,000

LO 3c

35  Touch plc is finalising certain figures that will appear in its financial statements as at 30 April 20X7. Relevant initial trial balance figures are as follows:

|  | £ |
| --- | --- |
| Trade and other payables (excluding interest payable) | 246,800 |
| 6% debentures as at 1 May 20X6 | 400,000 |

Touch plc issued 6% debentures of £120,000 at par on 1 February 20X7, repayable at par in ten years' time. No interest was outstanding at 1 May 20X6, and the company paid interest in respect of debentures of £24,000 in the period to 30 April 20X7.

The trade and other payables figure (including interest payable) that will appear in Touch plc's statement of financial position as at 30 April 20X7 is

A    £222,800

B    £246,800

C    £248,600

D    £272,600

LO 3c

36  As at 30 September 20X6 Madeley plc has a negative cash book balance of £2,643. Its bank statement shows a debit balance of £9,647. The following matters are discovered.

1    Madeley plc's cashier prepared a paying in slip with a total value of £5,016 and paid this into the bank on 30 September 20X6 with cash and cheques.  No amount in respect of this appears on the month-end bank statement. Madeley plc has since been notified by the bank that the paying in slip total was overcast by £90.

2    Madeley plc recorded and presented for payment at its bank a cheque for £1,988 from Reaney plc on 26 September 20X6, and this appeared on the bank statement on 27 September. On 30 September the bank statement shows that it was returned unpaid; Madeley plc was informed of this by letter on 1 October 20X6.

3    The company held notes and coin at 30 September 20X6 of £160.

In Madeley plc's statement of financial position as at 30 September 20X6 its figure for current liabilities in relation to the overdraft will be:

A    £565

B    £745

C    £4,721

D    £4,881

LO 2b, 3c

37  As at 1 June 20X4 Brazil plc had 400,000 10p equity shares, which it issued in 20X1 at £2.20 each, fully paid. It also had 200,000 £1 8% irredeemable preference shares issued at par in 20X2. On 31 January 20X5 Brazil plc made a further issue of 45,000 of the £1 irredeemable 8% preference shares at £1.50 fully paid. On the same date Brazil plc made a 1 for 4 bonus issue of equity shares. Brazil plc wishes to use the share premium account in respect of the bonus issue.

In its statement of financial position as at 31 May 20X5 Brazil plc will have share premium account of:

A  £452,500

B  £762,500

C  £830,000

D  £852,500

LO 1c, 1d, 3c

38  At 1 July 20X7 Leak plc owed £524,925 to suppliers plus £9,653 to staff in respect of bonuses. In the year to 30 June 20X8 it paid trade suppliers £1,249,506, and £34,682 in staff bonuses. Leak plc also posted £1,987,345 to its trade payables control account from the purchases day book, and received discounts of £12,824. At the end of the period it processed a contra with the receivables ledger of £8,236, and calculated that it owed staff bonuses of £12,762.

What amount of staff bonuses will be included in Leak plc's administrative expenses for the year ended 30 June 20X8?

A  £12,267

B  £31,573

C  £37,791

D  £57,097

LO 1c, 3c

1    What does GAAP stand for?

     A     Generally Agreed Accounting Policies

     B     Generally Accepted Accounting Policies

     C     Generally Agreed Accounting Practice

     D     Generally Accepted Accounting Practice

                                                     LO 3c

2    In the UK which of the following are responsible for the preparation of company annual financial statements?

     A     The shareholders

     B     The board of directors

     C     The auditors

     D     The members

                                                     LO 1a

3    Creditors falling due after more than one year are equivalent to current liabilities

     A     True

     B     False

     Non-current assets are equivalent to fixed assets

     C     True

     D     False

                                                       LO 3c

4    Teacup Ltd uses the first-in, first-out (FIFO) method to value its stocks of finished goods. At 1 January there were stocks of 25 units that had cost £54 each. During January the following transactions occurred:

     8 January        10 units were sold for £62 each
     15 January      10 units were purchased for £55 each
     22 January      10 units were sold for £62 each

     What was the value of Teacup Ltd's closing stock at 31 January?

     A     £815

     B     £810

     C     £825

     D     £820

                                                       LO 1c

5   Diamond Ltd issues 250,000 equity shares with a nominal value of £2 each at a price of £3.55 each for cash.

Which of the following sets of entries would be made to record this transaction?

A   Credit Bank £887,500, Debit Share capital £500,000, Debit Share premium £387,500

B   Debit Bank £887,500, Credit Share capital £250,000, Credit Share premium £637,500

C   Debit Bank £887,500, Credit Share capital £500,000, Credit Share premium £387,500

D   Credit Bank £887,500, Debit Share capital £250,000, Debit Share premium £637,500

LO 1c, 1d, 2d

6   The following balances have been extracted from Saracen Ltd's trial balance at 31 December 20X8:

|  | Debit £ | Credit £ |
|---|---|---|
| Retained profits at 1 January 20X8 | | 4,695,600 |
| 10% debentures issued in 20X5 | | 1,300,000 |
| Debenture interest paid | 65,000 | |

Operating profit for the year ended 31 December 20X8 is £520,000. Corporation tax for the year has been estimated at £156,000.

What is the figure for retained profits in Saracen Ltd's balance sheet as at the year end, 31 December 20X8?

A   £4,929,600

B   £4,994,600

C   £5,059,600

D   £5,215,600

LO 1c, 3c

7   Which of the following transactions would initially be recorded in a company's journal rather than its cash book?

A   Bonus issue of shares

B   Sale of goods for cash to a customer

C   Receipt of loan from a bank

D   Purchase for cash of shares in another company

LO 1b, 1c

8    At the end of its first year of trading on 30 June 20X1 Waddy Ltd's net assets are £207,594. It has share capital of £50,000 made up of 25p equity shares issued at 40p each, and a retained profits reserve of £107,594.

In relation to Waddy Ltd's balance sheet at 30 June 20X1 which of the following statements could be true?

A    It has a general reserve of £50,000

B    It has share premium of £100,000

C    It has a general reserve of £20,000

D    It has share premium of £50,000

LO 1c, 3a, 3c

1   Alice and Betty are in partnership, sharing profits and losses in the ratio 2:1. Their year end is 30 June.

On 1 January 20X4 Cath joined the partnership and the new profit sharing ratio became Alice 50%, Betty 30% and Cath 20%.

The profit for the year ended 30 June 20X4 was £520,000, after charging an expense of £40,000 which related to the first 6 months of the year. The remainder of the profit accrued evenly over the year.

What is Betty's total profit share for the year ended 30 June 20X4?

A   £173,333

B   £156,000

C   £164,666

D   £164,000

LO 1d

---

**The following information is relevant for questions 2 and 3**

Lisa, Mary and Olga are in partnership, sharing profits and losses in the ratio 30%, 30%, 40%. Their agreement states that Olga and Lisa are to receive annual salaries of £20,000 and £35,000 respectively. Interest credited on capital is 5% and interest charged on drawings is 10%. The following information is relevant.

|  | £ |
|---|---|
| Capital accounts at 31.12.X5 | |
| Lisa | 500,000 |
| Mary | 400,000 |
| Olga | 300,000 |
| Current accounts at 31.12.X4 | |
| Lisa | 300,000 |
| Mary | 150,000 |
| Olga | 400,000 |
| Drawings on 31.12.X5 | |
| Lisa | 70,000 |
| Mary | 35,000 |
| Olga | 40,000 |

Assume that drawings were made on the first day of the year for the purposes of calculating interest.

Net profit for the year ended 31.12.X5 was £1,350,000.

---

2   What is Olga's total share of the profits for the year ended 31.12.X5?

A   £391,350

B   £427,850

C   £529,000

D   £530,800

LO 1d

3   What is the closing balance on Mary's current account at 31.12.X5?

A   £390,500

B   £391,350

C   £506,350

D   £541,350

LO 1d

4   Declan and Indiah are in partnership, sharing profits 3:2.

On 1 July 20X4 Calum joins the partnership. Under the new partnership agreement profits will be shared by Declan, Indiah and Calum 5:3:2 respectively with the following annual salaries.

Indiah   £40,000 pa

Calum   £48,000 pa

Profit accrues evenly over the year. The partnership profit at 31 December 20X4 was £450,000.

At 31 December 20X4 how should the profits be allocated?

|   | Declan | Indiah | Calum |
|---|--------|--------|-------|
| A | £229,500 | £165,900 | £54,600 |
| B | £236,500 | £160,900 | £52,600 |
| C | £225,000 | £135,000 | £90,000 |
| D | £225,500 | £164,300 | £60,200 |

LO 1d

5   Billy and Charlie are in partnership together sharing profits equally. They invested £20,000 and £30,000 respectively in the business, although Billy later made a loan of £5,000 to the business. The loan is still outstanding. Interest is charged on capital and loans at 5% pa and is credited to current accounts.

The balances on the partners' current accounts at 1 April 20X5 were £15,500 for Billy and £12,700 for Charlie. The partnership made a profit of £32,000 for the year ending 31 March 20X6, before accruing for any interest.

What is the balance on the partners' current accounts at 31 March 20X6?

|   | Billy | Charlie |
|---|-------|---------|
| A | £31,500 | £28,700 |
| B | £31,375 | £28,825 |
| C | £31,625 | £28,825 |
| D | £31,250 | £28,950 |

LO 1d

6   Curtis and Sillett are in partnership, sharing profits 3:2 and compiling their accounts to 30 June each year.

On 1 January 20X6, McAllister joined the partnership, and from that date the profit sharing ratio became Curtis 50%, Sillett 25% and McAllister 25%, after providing for salaries for Sillett and McAllister of £20,000 and £12,000 pa respectively.

The partnership profit for the year ended 30 June 20X6 was £480,000, accruing evenly over the year.

What are the partners' total profit shares for the year ended 30 June 20X6?

|   | *Curtis* | *Sillett* | *McAllister* |
|---|---|---|---|
| A | £256,000 | £162,000 | £62,000 |
| B | £248,000 | £168,000 | £64,000 |
| C | £264,000 | £166,000 | £66,000 |
| D | £264,000 | £156,000 | £60,000 |

LO 1d

---

7   A partner's private petrol bills have been treated as part of the partnership's motor vehicle expenses. Which of the following journals corrects the error?

A   Debit Drawings account, Credit Motor vehicle expenses account

B   Debit Motor vehicle expenses account, Credit Drawings account

C   Debit Motor vehicle expenses account, Credit Capital account

D   Debit Capital account, Credit Motor vehicle expenses account

LO 1c, 1d, 2d

---

8   How should interest charged on partners' drawings be dealt with in partnership financial statements?

A   Credited as income in the income statement

B   Deducted from profit in allocating the profit among the partners

C   Added to profit in allocating the profit among the partners

D   Debited as an expense in the income statement.

LO 1c, 1d

---

9   Which of the following journals records interest earned on partners' capital account balances?

A   Debit Partners' current accounts, Credit Profit and loss appropriation account

B   Debit Profit and loss appropriation account, Credit Partners' current accounts

C   Debit Profit and loss appropriation account, Credit Cash at bank

D   Debit Profit and loss appropriation account, Credit Partners' capital accounts

LO 1c, 1d, 2d

10  P and Q are in partnership, sharing profits in the ratio 2:1. On 1 July 20X4 they admitted P's son R as a partner. P guaranteed that R's profit share would not be less than £25,000 for the six months to 31 December 20X4. The profit sharing arrangements after R's admission were P 50%, Q 30%, R 20%. The profit for the year ended 31 December 20X4 is £240,000, accruing evenly over the year.

What should P's final profit share be for the year ended 31 December 20X4?

A   £140,000

B   £139,000

C   £114,000

D   £139,375

LO 1c, 1d

11  What journal is necessary to record interest payable on partners' drawings?

A   Debit Partners' drawings accounts, Credit Partners' current accounts

B   Debit Profit and loss appropriation account, Credit Partners' drawings accounts

C   Debit Partners' drawings accounts, Credit Interest payable account

D   Debit Partners' current accounts, Credit Profit and loss appropriation account

LO 1c, 1d, 2d

12  Faith, Hope and Charity are partners sharing residual profits in the ratio 3:2:1. The partnership agreement provides for interest on capital at the rate of 8% per annum and a salary for Hope of £8,000 per annum. Net profit for 20X5 was £84,000 and the balances on partners' capital accounts throughout the year were: Faith £20,000; Hope £15,000; Charity £12,000.

What is Charity's share of residual profits for 20X5?

A   £12,040

B   £12,667

C   £13,000

D   £14,000

LO 1c, 1d, 2d

13  P, after having been a sole trader for some years, entered into partnership with Q on 1 July 20X2, sharing profits equally.

The business profit for the year ended 31 December 20X2 was £340,000, accruing evenly over the year, apart from a charge of £20,000 for a bad debt relating to trading before 1 July 20X2 which it was agreed that P should bear entirely.

How is the profit for the year to be divided between P and Q?

|   | P | Q |
|---|---|---|
| A | £245,000 | £95,000 |
| B | £250,000 | £90,000 |
| C | £270,000 | £90,000 |
| D | £255,000 | £85,000 |

LO 1c, 1d

14  G, H and I are in partnership, compiling their accounts for the year to 31 December each year.

The profit-sharing arrangements are as follows:

Until 30 June 20X3: annual salaries H: £40,000, I: £20,000, balance to be split 3:1:1.

From 1 July 20X3 salaries to be discontinued, profit to be divided 5: 3: 2.

The profit for the year ended 31 December 20X3 was £400,000 before charging partners' salaries, accruing evenly through the year and after charging an expense of £40,000 which it was agreed related wholly to the first six months of the year.

How should the profit for the year be divided among the partners?

|   | G | H | I |
|---|---|---|---|
| A | £182,000 | £130,000 | £88,000 |
| B | £200,000 | £116,000 | £84,000 |
| C | £198,000 | £118,000 | £88,000 |
| D | £180,000 | £132,000 | £88,000 |

LO 1c, 1d

---

15  X and Y are in partnership, sharing profits in the ratio 2:1 and compiling their financial statements to 30 June each year.

On 1 January 20X4 Z joined the partnership, and it was agreed that the profit-sharing arrangement should become X 50%, Y 30% and Z 20%.

The profit for the year ended 30 June 20X4 was £540,000, after charging an expense of £30,000 which it was agreed related to the period before 1 January 20X4. The profit otherwise accrued evenly over the year.

What is X's total profit share for the year ended 30 June 20X4?

A    £305,000

B    £312,500

C    £315,000

D    £295,000

LO 1c, 1d

---

16  G, H and I are in partnership, sharing profits in the ratio 3:1:1, after charging salaries of £20,000 per year each for H and I. On 1 January 20X4 they agreed to change the profit-sharing ratio to 3:2:1 and to discontinue H's salary. I's salary continued unchanged. The partnership profit for the year ended 30 June 20X4 was £380,000, accruing evenly over the year.

How should the £380,000 profit be divided among the partners?

|   | G | H | I |
|---|---|---|---|
| A | £192,000 | £104,000 | £84,000 |
| B | £192,500 | £103,333 | £84,167 |
| C | £209,000 | £101,333 | £69,667 |
| D | £179,000 | £111,333 | £89,667 |

LO 1c, 1d

17  The current account of a partner has been written up as follows.

CURRENT ACCOUNT

|  | £ |  | £ |
|---|---|---|---|
| Interest on capital | 2,800 | Balance b/d | 270 |
| Salary | 1,500 | Drawings | 6,200 |
| Balance c/d | 10,870 | Profit share | 8,700 |
|  | 15,170 |  | 15,170 |

The balance brought down is entered correctly and the other entries are all correct in amount.

What is the correct balance carried down?

A    A debit balance of £1,530

B    A debit balance of £6,530

C    A credit balance of £7,070

D    A credit balance of £16,470

LO 1c, 1d

18  A sole trader's trial balance totals were:

| Debit | £387,642 |
|---|---|
| Credit | £379,642 |

A suspense account was opened for the difference.

Which of the following errors would have the effect of reducing the difference when corrected?

A    The bank deposit balance of £8,000 has been omitted from the trial balance

B    £4,000 received for rent of part of the office has been correctly recorded in the cash book and debited to Rent account

C    No entry has been made in the records for a cash sale of £8,000

D    £8,000 paid for repairs to plant has been debited to the plant asset account

LO 2a, 2b

19  A sole trader's trial balance at 31 October 20X9 does not agree, with the debit side totalling £500 less than the credit side. During November, the following errors are discovered:

1    The sales day book for October had been undercast by £150

2    Rent received of £240 had been credited to the rent payable account from the cash book

3    The allowance for receivables, which decreased by £420, had been recorded in the allowance for receivables account as an increase

Following the correction of these errors, the balance on the suspense account would be

A    £340 credit

B    £250 credit

C    £1,340 debit

D    £340 debit

LO 2a, 2b

20 A trial balance extracted from a sole trader's records failed to agree, and a suspense account was opened for the difference.

Which of the following matters would require an entry in the suspense account to correct them?

A    Discount allowed was mistakenly debited to discount received account.

B    Cash received from the sale of a non-current asset was correctly entered in the cash book and was credited to the disposal account.

C    The balance on the rent account was omitted from the trial balance.

D    Goods taken from inventory by the owner had been recorded by crediting Drawings account and debiting Purchases account.

LO 2a, 2b

21 A gas accrual for £400 at the reporting date was treated as a prepayment in a sole trader's financial statements. As a result the profit was

A    Understated by £800

B    Understated by £400

C    Overstated by £800

D    Overstated by £400

LO 2a

22 A sole trader prepares financial statements each year to 31 May. His rent is payable quarterly in advance on 1 January, 1 April, 1 July and 1 October. Local property taxes are paid each year in two equal instalments on 1 April and 1 October.

His annual rental for the calendar years 20X6 and 20X7 was £4,800 and £5,400 respectively but on 1 January 20X8 this was increased to £6,600 per annum. Local property tax for the last three years has been as follows:

|  | £ |
|---|---|
| Year commencing 1 April 20X6 | 3,600 |
| Year commencing 1 April 20X7 | 3,900 |
| Year commencing 1 April 20X8 | 4,500 |

In preparing his financial statements for the year ended 31 May 20X8, the charge to the profit and loss account from his rent and local property tax account would be

A    £9,900

B    £10,100

C    £10,200

D    £10,300

LO 1c, 3c

23 On 1 April 20X0 a sole trader paid £3,080 in local taxes for the year ending 31 March 20X1. This was an increase of 10% on the charge for the previous year.

What is the correct charge for local taxes in her profit and loss account for the year ended 31 December 20X0?

A £2,870

B £3,003

C £3,010

D £3,080

LO 1c, 3c

24 A local taxes prepayment of £475 at the reporting date was treated as an accrual in preparing a trader's profit and loss account. As a result, his profit was

A Understated by £950

B Overstated by £950

C Understated by £475

D Overstated by £475

LO 2a

25 The net assets of Walter's business decreased by £11,025 over the year to 31 October 20X7. During that year he had paid in additional capital of £14,000, drawn £875 in cash each month and, on one occasion, taken goods costing £2,625 for his own use.

The loss made by the business for the year ended 31 October 20X7 was

A £10,150

B £11,900

C £21,525

D £25,025

LO 1c, 1d, 3a

26 Harry has been unable to calculate his business' profit or loss for the year ended 31 December 20X8 as fire destroyed most of his accounting records. He has, however, been able to provide the following information.

(1) Net assets at 31 December 20X7 were £23,000 and £32,500 at 31 December 20X8

(2) He introduced capital during the year of £4,000 cash

(3) He took cash drawings of £2,500 and goods with a selling price of £800. The cost of the goods was £750.

What was Harry's profit or loss for the year ended 31 December 20X8?

A £8,750 profit

B £(1,750) loss

C £9,800 profit

D £(2,750) loss

LO 1c, 1d, 3a

27 Alexander's net assets have increased by £127,000 over the year. He took drawings of £47,000 and paid in the proceeds of a personal life insurance policy amounting to £25,000. His net profit for the year was

A £55,000

B £105,000

C £149,000

D £199,000

LO 1c, 1d, 3a

28 A business has net assets of £286,400 on 31 January 20X6 and had net assets of £266,800 on 31 January 20X5. During the year the owner of the business

(1) took goods for his own use which cost £10,000 and had a market value of £14,000

(2) introduced capital of £50,000

(3) withdrew £30,000 as salary.

The profit for the year was

A £9,600

B £30,400

C £70,400

D £109,600

LO 1c, 1d, 3a

29 Which TWO of the following would be classified as current liabilities in the balance sheet of a sole trader?

A   Owner's capital

B   Accrued interest charges

C   Drawings

D   Bank overdraft

E   Income tax payable

LO 3c

30 Which of the following equations represents the closing capital of a sole trader?

A   Opening capital – capital introduced + profit – drawings

B   Opening capital – capital introduced – profit + drawings

C   Opening capital + capital introduced + profit – drawings

D   Opening capital + capital introduced – loss + drawings

LO 1d, 3a, 3c

31 Sayhan, Errol and Alev are in partnership, preparing financial statements as at 31 August each year and sharing profits 4:3:1. Sayhan retired on 30 April 20X2, and Errol and Alev continued, sharing profits 3:1 respectively.

Goodwill as at 30 April 20X2 (not to be retained in the accounts) was valued at £50,000. The net entry to Errol's capital account to include and then eliminate goodwill is

A   Debit £6,250

B   Debit £18,750

C   Credit £6,250

D   Credit £18,750

LO 1d

32 Samantha, a sole trader, does not keep a debtors control account or a sales day book and is not registered for VAT. The bookkeeper has discovered the following errors and omissions in Samantha's accounting records:

(1)  a cheque for £180 from a customer has been returned unpaid by the bank. No entries have been made in the accounting records for the return of the cheque

(2)  a credit note for £12 was sent to a customer but was mistaken for an invoice by Samantha's accounts clerk when recording it

Which of the following journals will be entered in Samantha's nominal ledger accounts in order to correct these items?

A   Debit Debtors £156, Debit Sales £24, Credit Cash £180

B   Debit Cash £180, Credit Debtors £156, Credit Sales £24

C   Debit Debtors £168, Debit Sales £12, Credit Cash £180

D   Debit Bad debts expense £180, Debit Debtors £24, Credit Cash £180, Credit Sales £24

LO 1c, 2d

33 Which THREE of the following could be found in the financial statements of a partnership?

A Fixed assets

B Share premium

C Drawings

D Dividends paid

E Profit for the year

LO 3c

34 Sunil started business on 1 December 20X3 with cash of £5,000. He has not yet prepared a full set of financial statements. As at the end of his first reporting period, 30 November 20X4, he has cash at bank of £1,726. He made sales of £33,498 during the period and paid expenses in cash of £19,385. He has no outstanding creditors at the end of the period, and has no fixed assets or stock, but one customer owes him £2,387.

Assuming Sunil made no other capital injections but took drawings of £15,000 in the period, identify his profit for the 12 month reporting period to 30 November 20X4 and his net assets at the end of the period on an accrual basis.

A Net profit of £11,726, net assets of £1,726

B Net profit of £14,113, net assets of £4,113

C Net profit of £11,726, net assets of £4,113

D Net profit of £14,113, net assets of £1,726

LO 1c, 3b

35 Sayhan, Errol and Alev are in partnership, preparing financial statements as at 31 August each year and sharing profits 4:3:1. Sayhan retired on 30 April 20X2, and Errol and Alev continued, sharing profits 3:1 respectively.

The business's profit for appropriation (arising evenly over the 12 months to 31 August 20X2) was £121,248. For the year to 31 August 20X2 Errol's profit share is

A £30,312

B £45,468

C £60,624

D £90,936

LO 1d

36 Leonard's initial trial balance as at 30 April 20X9 has already been entered on the extended trial balance for the period. Leonard's drawings of £38,100 in total have been debited to the other expenses account in error. In the adjustments columns on his extended trial balance Leonard should make TWO entries of £38,100:

A Debit the capital account

B Credit the capital account

C Debit the other expenses account

D Credit the other expenses account

LO 2c

37    On her extended trial balance, Hermione's final net profit figure will appear in which TWO of the following columns?

    A    Debit column of the profit and loss account

    B    Credit column of the profit and loss account

    C    Debit column of the balance sheet

    D    Credit column of the balance sheet

LO 2c

---

38    Helen, John and Chris are in partnership, preparing financial statements as at 31 January each year and sharing profits 5:3:2.  Helen retired on 30 September 20X6, and John and Chris continued, sharing profits 5:3 respectively.  Goodwill as at 30 September 20X6 (not to be retained in the accounts) was valued at £50,000.  The net entry to John's capital account to include and then eliminate goodwill is:

    A    Debit £3,750

    B    Debit £16,250

    C    Credit £3,750

    D    Credit £16,250

LO 1d

---

39    Ines, Alex and Sebastian are in partnership sharing profits 3:2:1. Each partner has a combined capital and current account, which at 1 July 20X7 were as follows:

Ines          £10,490

Alex          £12,020

Sebastian    £20,170

During the year to 30 June 20X8 the partnership made profits of £87,750, and each partner took drawings of £7,500. On 30 June 20X8 Alex retires. The partners value goodwill at £60,000 at that date, but do not wish this valuation to remain in the accounts. Ines and Sebastian will continue in partnership, sharing profits equally.

What is the balance on Sebastian's capital and current account on 1 July 20X8?

    A    £46,865

    B    £14,795

    C    £53,770

    D    £7,295

LO 1d

40 Shula and Kenton are in partnership sharing profits and losses 5:3 after allowing for partner salaries of £20,000 and £25,000 respectively. On 1 November 20X8 Shula lent the business £50,000 at 8% interest pa. The net profit for the year ended 30 April 20X9, before loan interest, is £122,000.

How much profit will be credited to Kenton's current account?

A £53,875

B £66,875

C £53,125

D £52,375

LO 1d, 2c

41 Burgess does not keep a creditors control account nor a purchases day book. Burgess's bookkeeper has discovered that, in respect of an invoice for £2,606 from Lever, total settlement discount of £52 was available. In error two cheques were sent to the supplier, both in settlement of the invoice. The first cheque was for £2,606 and the second was for £2,554. Both cheques were cashed by Lever. The first cheque was fully recorded by Burgess; the second cheque was recorded only in the payments column of Burgess's cash book.

Which of the following journals will be entered in Burgess's nominal ledger accounts in order to correct these items?

A Debit Lever £2,554, Credit Suspense £2,554

B Debit Cash £2,606, Credit Lever £2,554, Credit Discounts received £52

C Debit Suspense £2,554, Debit Discounts received £52, Credit Lever £2,606

D Debit Lever £2,606, Credit Suspense £2,554, Credit Discounts received £52

LO 2b, 2d

42 In relation to accounting for partnerships, which TWO of the following statements are true?

A Goods taken by a partner from the business are treated as drawings

B Interest on drawings by a partner is income in the partnership's profit and loss account

C Interest on a partner's loan capital is income in the partnership's profit and loss account

D Drawings by a partner are credited in the current account

E In the absence of a partnership agreement, no salaries are due to partners

LO 1d

43 In a partnership, interest on partners' drawings affects

A net profit available for appropriation only

B the cash position only

C neither net profit available for appropriation nor the cash position

D both net profit available for appropriation and the cash position

LO 1d

44 Ben and Josh went into business together on 1 March 20X2 without a formal partnership agreement. At that date Ben contributed £10,000 fixed capital to the business and Josh contributed £20,000 fixed capital. On 1 December 20X2 Josh made a loan to the partnership of £40,000.

To how much, if any, interest are the partners together entitled in respect of their capital and loan for the year ended 28 February 20X3?

A £2,000

B £1,000

C £500

D £Nil

LO 1d

---

45 Randolph started a trading business on 1 May 20X4 with capital of £40,000. In his first year of trading he made a net profit of £117,000, selling goods at a mark-up on cost of 60%. He injected additional capital of £30,000 in the year and withdrew a monthly amount of £3,200 for his living expenses. He also took drawings from stock of goods with a resale value of £7,200. He had no stock at the year end.

What were Randolph's net assets at 30 April 20X5?

A £141,400

B £144,100

C £144,280

D £179,300

LO 3a

---

46 Mushtaq, a sole trader, has the following information at the start and end of his second year of trading.

| | At 31 December 20X0 £ | At 1 January 20X0 £ |
|---|---|---|
| Fixed assets (net book value) | 46,000 | 39,400 |
| Stock | 18,900 | 15,600 |
| Trade debtors | 8,400 | 11,500 |
| Trade creditors | 7,500 | 10,200 |
| Cash in hand | 6,400 | 6,600 |

During 20X0 Mushtaq introduced £3,000 capital. He took stock for his own use that cost £500, and paid himself £750 per month.

What is Mushtaq's profit or loss for 20X0?

A £15,800 profit

B £2,800 loss

C £16,300 profit

D £18,800 profit

LO 3a

47  Part of the process of preparing a sole trader's cash flow statement is the calculation of cash inflow from operating activities.

Which of the following statements about that calculation (using the indirect method) are correct?

1   Loss on sale of operating fixed assets should be deducted from operating profits.

2   Increase in stock should be deducted from operating profits.

3   Increase in creditors should be added to operating profits.

4   Depreciation charges should be added to operating profits.

A   1, 2 and 3

B   1, 2 and 4

C   1, 3 and 4

D   2, 3 and 4

LO 3c

---

48  In the course of preparing a sole trader's cash flow statement, the following figures are to be included in the calculation of net cash from operating activities.

|  | £ |
|---|---|
| Depreciation charges | 980,000 |
| Profit on sale of fixed assets | 40,000 |
| Increase in stocks | 130,000 |
| Decrease in debtors | 100,000 |
| Increase in creditors | 80,000 |

What will the net effect of these items be in the cash flow statement?

|  |  | £ |
|---|---|---|
| A | Addition to operating profit | 890,000 |
| B | Subtraction from operating profit | 890,000 |
| C | Addition to operating profit | 1,070,000 |
| D | Addition to operating profit | 990,000 |

LO 3c

---

49  Part of a draft cash flow statement is shown below:

|  | £000 |
|---|---|
| Operating profit | 8,640 |
| Depreciation charges | (2,160) |
| Proceeds of sale of fixed assets | 360 |
| Increase in stock | (330) |
| Increase in creditors | 440 |

The following criticisms of the above extract have been made:

1   Depreciation charges should have been added, not deducted.

2   Increase in stock should have been added, not deducted.

3   Increase in creditors should have been deducted, not added.

4   Proceeds of sale of fixed assets should not appear in this part of the cash flow statement.

Which of these criticisms are valid?

A    2 and 3 only

B    1 and 4 only

C    1 and 3 only

D    2 and 4 only

LO 3c

50   Which of the following assertions about cash flow statements is/are correct?

1    A cash flow statement prepared using the direct method produces a different figure for net cash flow from operating activities to that produced when the indirect method is used.

2    Rights issues of shares do not feature in cash flow statements.

3    A bonus issue will not appear as an item in a cash flow statement.

4    A profit on the sale of a fixed asset will appear as an item under Capital Expenditure in a cash flow statement.

A    1 and 4

B    2 and 3

C    3 only

D    2 and 4

LO 3c

51   An extract from a cash flow statement prepared by a trainee accountant is shown below.

Cash flows from operating activities

|  | £m |
| --- | --- |
| Net profit before taxation | 28 |
| Adjustments for: Depreciation | (9) |
| Operating profit before working capital changes | 19 |
| Decrease in stocks | 13 |
| Increase in debtors | (4) |
| Increase in creditors | (8) |
| Cash generated from operations | 10 |

Which of the following criticisms of this extract are correct?

1    Depreciation charges should have been added, not deducted

2    Decrease in stocks should have been deducted, not added.

3    Increase in debtors should have been added, not deducted.

4    Increase in creditors should have been added, not deducted

A    2 and 4

B    2 and 3

C    1 and 3

D    1 and 4

LO 3c

# Answer Bank

1   C   Capital expenditure relates to the acquisition of, or improvement of the earning capacity of, non-current assets.

2   D   Legal fees incurred on the purchase of a building – the others are all revenue expenditure.

3   B   £400 spent on purchasing a new PC to replace his secretary's old one. Item A is drawings, C is the acquisition of a current asset in the form of inventory, and D is a revenue expense.

4   D   Information's relevance is affected by its materiality. A, B and C are all characteristics contributing to information being a faithful representation of what it purports to represent.

5   A   This is set out in paragraph QC19 of the *Conceptual Framework*.

6   B,C,E

    The employees, the bank and the suppliers will be interested.

    Neither stock market analysts nor institutional shareholders (large owners of company shares eg pension funds) would be interested in investing in a small private company.

7   A,C   Both tax and national statistics will apply to the needs of government and its agencies. Whether the business will continue as a going concern (B) is an issue for the sole trader, its suppliers, customers and employees. Probably only the sole trader is interested in their own stewardship (D) of the business's resources; this is really only an issue for company owners, as is (E).                                                    SAMPLE PAPER (amended)

8   B   The financial position of an entity is reflected in the resources it controls (assets), financial structure (debt and capital), liquidity (cash) and solvency (ability to pay its debts). Most of this information is provided in the statement of financial position (B).

    The income statement primarily provides information about an entity's financial performance, while the statement of cash flows reflects changes in the financial position. Retained earnings is a figure in the statement of financial position which accumulates movements over the years in retained earnings.

9   A,D   The *Conceptual Framework* states that information about the economic resources (A) and claims (D) of an entity can help users to identify the reporting entity's financial strengths and weaknesses. That information can then be used to help users to assess the reporting entity's liquidity and solvency.

10   A,C   International Accounting Standard 1 (IAS 1) *Presentation of Financial Statements* (revised) provides the objective of financial statements. It states that the objective of financial statements is to provide information about the financial position, financial performance and cash flows of an entity that is useful to a wide range of users in making economic decisions (C). In addition it states that the financial statements also show the results of management's stewardship of the resources entrusted to it (A).

11   C   1 and 4 only. Financial information can make a difference to decisions if it has predictive value (it can be used to predict future outcomes) or confirmatory value (it provides feedback about previous evaluations).

12   D   The historical cost convention

13   C   Profit will be overstated due to depreciation based on understated assets, and cost of sales based on understated inventory.

14   D   Substance over form means that the economic substance of an item should be reflected rather than its strict legal form (A). Recognition of items on the basis of monetary amounts is the money measurement concept, not the historical cost concept (B). Items should not be excluded on the basis of being difficult to understand (C).

15  D  (1)  Information must be **both** relevant and faithfully represented to be useful

       (2)  Materiality concerns whether an item in the financial statements can influence users' decisions; there is no absolute amount that makes an item material

       (3)  Substance over form means that the commercial effect should be recognised, not the strict legal form

16  D  Definitions per IAS 1 (revised)

17  A  According to IAS 1 (revised) paragraph 25, going concern relates to whether the entity will continue in operational existence without liquidating, ceasing trading or being unable to avoid these things (A).

SAMPLE PAPER

18  D  IAS 1 (revised) paragraph 15

SAMPLE PAPER

19  C  Omissions or misstatements of items are material (C) if they could, individually or collectively, influence the economic decisions of users taken on the basis of the financial statements (IAS 1). It is the information in the financial statements as a whole that should be neutral ie free from bias (A). Prudence (B) is the inclusion of a degree of caution when making judgements in relation to estimates. Understandable (D) is an enhancing characteristic mentioned in the *Conceptual Framework* concerned with classifying, characterising and presenting information clearly and concisely.

1   C   The accounting equation Assets = Opening capital + profit – drawings + liabilities can be rewritten as: Assets – liabilities – opening capital + drawings = profit

2   D   Petrol being paid in petty cash means assets decrease and drawings increase, which decrease capital. Option A is a switch between assets, while options B and C increase assets and increase liabilities.

3   C   The lengthening of the period of credit given to customers, since this means that while there are increased profits as the level of sales increases, it takes longer to collect cash from those customers.

4   D   A relates to the income statement, B and C suggest that the statement of financial position represents a valuation which is incorrect, while D is correct in that it is the definition of a statement of financial position's purpose.

5   A   The overdraft liability will decrease and receivables will decrease by an equal amount.

6   A   Assets will increase as the sole trader has acquired inventory, and liabilities will increase as the goods were purchased on credit.

7   A   Assets increase as cash on receipt of the loan funds, and liabilities will increase as the loan is a liability.

8   B   Assets will increase as there is an increase in cash of £500 and a decrease in inventory of only £300, and capital will increase due to the profit of £200

9   C   The car increases assets while it is treated as capital introduced rather than as a liability of the business to its proprietor.

10  A,B,G

   According to the *Conceptual Framework*, income, expenses and equity are elements of financial statements. The *Conceptual Framework* also identifies assets and liabilities as elements of financial statements.

1    C    12,450 + 2,480 + 1,350 = £16,280

2    A    True

     D    False (the cash book is the book of original entry for discounts)

3    B    The exact amount of petty cash expenditure is reimbursed at intervals to maintain a fixed float

4    B    A, C and D are all ledgers to which transactions are posted from the books of original entry. The journal (B) is the book of original entry that is used for unusual transactions and to correct errors and omissions.

5    D    50,000 + 17,000 + 7,500 + 6,000 = £80,500

6    B, D  Purchase order and goods received note

7    C    A credit note is issued by a supplier when a customer returns goods to them (C). Invoices (A) are issued when goods are originally sold, on the basis of a delivery note (D) which shows what exactly has been sold. A remittance advice (B) is sent in by the customer to the supplier with payment.

8    C    Discounts allowed, like discounts received, are recorded in the cash book as the book of original entry.

9    A    VAT on credit sales is recorded in the sales day book (A). VAT on cash sales and on credit purchases would be recorded in the cash book (C) and purchases day book respectively.

10   C    When purchases are made from a supplier with which the business does not have an account, they must be paid for in cash – so the book of original entry is the cash book.

11   A    There is £10 or a petty cash voucher for £10 missing from the petty cash box.

12   B    38,600 + 3,500 = £42,100

13   B, D  The invoice to a customer will be recorded in the sales day book while the cheque to a supplier will be recorded in the cash book. The purchase order and goods received note act as supporting documentation when an invoice arrives from a supplier, but are not themselves recorded in the books of original entry.  Similarly the delivery note acts as supporting documentation when preparing an invoice to a customer, but is not separately recorded.

14   A, F  Note that the question is asking about Johan plc's books of original entry, not Marius plc's. When Marius plc buys goods on credit, Johan plc sells them to it so only the sales day book (A) can be at issue. Contra entries are made in ledger accounts, not books of original entry, so only the payables ledger (F) can be at issue here.

SAMPLE PAPER

1   C   Dr Receivables £5,760, Cr Sales £4,800, Cr VAT £960

2   C   Options A and B are ruled out because they relate to rental *income*, which would be a credit (not a debit) in a rent account. Option D is ruled out because there is no entry made in the bank account and therefore no payment can yet have been made.

3   B   Debit entries decrease income and increase assets. Credit entries increase income, decrease assets and increase liabilities.

4   D

### VAT ACCOUNT

|  | £ |  | £ |
|---|---|---|---|
| Input tax | 176,949 | Output tax | 228,816 |
| Purchases (8,301 x 2) | 16,602 |  |  |
| Balance | 42,477 | Sales (3,606 x 2) | 7,212 |
|  | 236,028 |  | 236,028 |

5   B   False. A Ltd owes to B Ltd.

6   B   Debit payables, credit discounts received

7   A

### PAYABLES

|  | £ |  | £ |
|---|---|---|---|
| Payments (bal fig) | 212,130 | Bal b/d | 24,183 |
| Bal c/d | 34,655 | Purchases (254,192 – 31,590) | 222,602 |
|  | 246,785 |  | 246,785 |
|  |  | Bal b/d | 34,655 |

8   B   The payables ledger column in the cash payments book is debited to the payables account not the purchases account (A). The cash receipt recorded in the petty cash book when the petty cash is topped up is recorded as a credit entry in the main cash book, not a debit (C). VAT on cash book purchases is debited to the VAT account (D).

9   B   The correct double entry for discounts received from suppliers is to debit payables (reducing what is owed) and credit discounts received.

10   C   Cash paid to suppliers would be debited to payables and credited to cash (C). The purchases day book total (A) would be credited to payables (increasing the amount owed) and the cash purchases total (B) would not appear at all in the payables account. Discounts allowed (D) affect receivables, not payables.

11   B   Remember a trade discount is given by a manufacturer to a retailer, as opposed to a settlement discount, which is given for paying within a certain period of time.

12   A   The correct entry is to record the expense and reduce the amount owed by customers: debit discount allowed, credit receivables.

13   A   (£950 – £50) x 20% = £180. Remember that for VAT purposes it is assumed the settlement discount will be claimed.

1　B　Inventories

2　C　Land is a non-current asset for long term use in the business.

3　D　Profit increases capital so it is credited to the statement of financial position column, and debited to the income statement column on the ETB.

4　D　A loss decreases capital so it is debited to the capital account in the statement of financial position, therefore the other side of the entry is to credit it to the profit and loss ledger account.

5　B

RECEIVABLES ACCOUNT

|  | £ |  | £ |
|---|---|---|---|
| Opening balance | 2,700 | Cash received | 15,300 |
| Credit sales | 16,500 | Closing balance | 3,900 |
|  | 19,200 |  | 19,200 |

6　A, D　Assets and expenses are debit balances; liabilities, capital and income are credit balances.

7　A　Drawings decrease capital so they are a debit (B); discount allowed and carriage outwards are expenses so they too are debits (C) and (D). A bank overdraft is a liability so it is a credit (A).

8　A　The opening inventories balance is included in the initial trial balance – the closing inventory (B) is not known until the inventory count and valuation has taken place. Owner's drawings are taken in the year and appear as a debit balance on the ITB (C). Non-current assets appear in the debit column of the statement of financial position on the ETB (D). A balanced ITB may still contain compensating errors and errors of principle or commission (A).

9　C

|  | £ |
|---|---|
| Revenue | 89,400 |
| Purchases (69,600 x 5/6) | (58,000) |
| Gross profit | 31,400 (C) |

Option A uses the cash paid figure, which includes VAT, as the cost of purchases. Option B assumes that the revenue figure is the gross one, whereas revenue in the income statement (and turnover in the profit and loss account, if this were a UK GAAP question) should be shown exclusive of VAT; it also uses the cash paid figure as the cost of purchases. Option D uses the correct VAT exclusive purchases figure, but again assumes the revenue figure includes VAT.

1  B  A supplier's invoice for £32 recorded as £23 in the purchases account, which is a transposition error in the nominal ledger. In (A) we are still recording a Dr and Cr. The payables ledger does not affect the trial balance as it is a memorandum account (C) and in (D) neither side of the entry will be recorded.

2  B  £4,410 credit

| CASH BOOK | | | |
|---|---|---|---|
| | £ | | £ |
| Balance c/d | 5,380 | ∴ Balance b/d | 4,410 |
| | | Standing order | 890 |
| | | Interest | 80 |
| | 5,380 | | 5,380 |

| | £ |
|---|---|
| Balance per bank statement | (5,250) |
| Less: unpresented cheques | (1,070) |
| Add: outstanding lodgements | 1,240 |
| Less: bank error | (300) |
| Balance per amended cash book | (5,380) |

3  A

| RECEIVABLES CONTROL | | | |
|---|---|---|---|
| | £ | | £ |
| Balance b/d | 414,000 | Cash from credit customers | 111,000 |
| Credit sales | 101,000 | Contras | 6,650 |
| | | Discounts | 1,400 |
| | | Irrecoverable debts | 13,600 |
| | | Balance c/d | 382,350 |
| | 515,000 | | 515,000 |

4  A  £1,800

| | £ |
|---|---|
| Balance per bank statement | (1,500) |
| Less unpresented cheque | (500) |
| Add uncredited lodgement | 200 |
| Cash at bank balance | (1,800) |

5  D  Bank overdraft of £3,591 was included in the trial balance as a debit. The difference results in a suspense account balance of £7,182 CR. Omitting a debit balance (prepayments) would make the credit total bigger than the debit total (A). In (B) the DR has been posted, just to the wrong account. Therefore there will be no impact on the trial balance totals. For (C) as neither entry has been posted the trial balance totals will still balance.

6  A  True

   D  False

7  A  True

   C  True

8  A  In the trial balance, both purchases and payables would be overstated by £260, but the overall totals for the debit and credit columns would agree.

**9    B**

Note the correct balance on the receivables ledger listing is 63,620 – (210 x 2) = 63,200

RECEIVABLES CONTROL ACCOUNT

|  | £ |  | £ |
|---|---|---|---|
| B/d | 65,000 | SDB overcast | 300 |
|  |  | Contra | 1,500 |
|  |  | ∴ c/d | 63,200 |
|  | 65,000 |  | 65,000 |

**10    B, C**    Cash book: direct debit on bank statement only (B), bank charges (C)

Deposits credited after date (A), bank error (D) and cheque presented after date (E) would appear on the bank reconciliation.

**11    A**

PAYABLES CONTROL ACCOUNT

|  | £ |  | £ |
|---|---|---|---|
| Cash | 2,500 | Bal b/d | 3,200 |
| Returns | 750 |  |  |
| Bal c/d | 3,250 | Purchases | 3,300 |
|  | 6,500 |  | 6,500 |

**12    A**    For the other items the trial balance will balance because: Drawings and sundry expenses are both debits (B), Both debits and credits suffer an omission in (C), capital expenditure and repairs are both debits (D).

**13    A**    The payment should have been debited not credited so the credit side is too high by £400. In (B) discount received £200 has been debited when it should have been credited, so debits are £400 higher. (C) has no effect on the TB balancing. (D) means that credits are too high, but only by £200.

**14    D**    £58,440 credit.

– £73,680 + 102,480 – 87,240 = 58,440 overdrawn.

**15    B**    As the receivables ledger is not part of the nominal ledger a transposition error made when posting cash received from a credit customer to it does not affect the nominal ledger.

**16    A**

PAYABLES CONTROL ACCOUNT

|  | £ |  | £ |
|---|---|---|---|
| Cash paid to suppliers | 494,200 | Opening balance | 192,300 |
| Contras | 2,100 | Purchases | 481,600 |
| Discounts received | 6,300 | Cash refunds | 8,700 |
| Balance c/d | 180,000 |  |  |
|  | 682,600 |  | 682,600 |

**17    D**    A cheque paid should be debited to an asset or expense account. In (A) and (C) if the discounts columns of the cash book were wrongly totalled this would affect both the debit and the credit when posted. In (B) cash paid for the purchase of office furniture was debited to the general expenses account – both a debit and a credit have been made even though the debit was to the wrong account.

**18    C**    (565) – 92 = (657). The cheque for £57 is already included in the cash book.

**19    B**    The discount received should have been credited to discounts received, so the effect is doubled. (A) would result in the credit side being £800 too high. (C) would have no effect at all. In (D) the credit side would be too high

**20    B**    This is an error of original entry.

**21  C**

| | £ |
|---|---|
| Cash book balance b/f | (8,970) |
| Bank charges | (550) |
| Correct cash book | (9,520) |
| Error | 425 |
| Unpresented cheques | 3,275 |
| Uncredited lodgements | (5,380) |
| Bank statement balance | (11,200) |

**22  D**

| | £ |
|---|---|
| Balance b/d | (5,675) |
| Add: standing order | 125 |
| Less: dishonoured cheque (450 × 2) | (900) |
| | (6,450) |

**23  A, D** Note that bank charges in the bank statement would be credited to the cash book, not debited

**24  A, E** The transactions should both have been debited. In (B), (C) and (D) the double entry is complete though not correct.

**25  C**

| | £ |
|---|---|
| Alpha balance | 4,140 |
| Discount disallowed | 40 |
| Cash paid | 4,080 |
| Goods returned | 380 |
| | 8,640 |
| Beta balance | 8,950 |
| Difference remaining | 310 |

**26  B**

| | £ |
|---|---|
| Balance per bank statement | (800) |
| Unpresented cheque | (80) |
| Doubtful cheque | – |
| | (880) |

**27  B**  Start by posting the adjustment in full:

| | Debit | Credit |
|---|---|---|
| | £ | £ |
| Discount allowed | 3,840 | 2,960 |
| Discount received | 3,840 | 2,960 |
| Suspense account | | 1,760 |

**28  A**

PAYABLES CONTROL ACCOUNT

| | £ | | £ |
|---|---|---|---|
| Cash paid to suppliers | 1,405,500 | Opening balance | 318,600 |
| Discounts received | 8,200 | Purchases | 1,268,600 |
| Contras | 48,000 | Refunds received from suppliers | 2,700 |
| Closing balance | 128,200 | | |
| | 1,589,900 | | 1,589,900 |

**29  A**  £8,500 – (2 x £400) = £7,700

**30  B**

| | £ |
|---|---|
| Original cash book figure | 2,490 |
| Adjustment re charges | (50) |
| Adjustment re dishonoured cheque | (140) |
| | 2,300 |

**31 C**

### RECEIVABLES CONTROL ACCOUNT

| | £ | | £ |
|---|---|---|---|
| Opening balance | 318,650 | Cash from customers | 181,140 |
| Credit sales | 157,780 | Discounts allowed | 1,240 |
| Refunds to credit customers | 280 | Irrecoverable debts written off | 1,390 |
| | | Closing balance | 292,940 |
| | 476,710 | | 476,710 |

**32 B**

### RECEIVABLES CONTROL ACCOUNT

| | £ | | £ |
|---|---|---|---|
| Opening balance | 180,000 | Cash from credit customers | 228,000 |
| Credit sales | 182,000 | Irrecoverable debts written off | 1,500 |
| Cash refunds | 3,300 | Discount allowed | 4,200 |
| | | Contras | 2,400 |
| | | Closing balance | 129,200 |
| | 365,300 | | 365,300 |

**33 A,B,D**

A represents unpresented cheques, and B and D represent uncredited lodgements. These are always included in the reconciliation of the bank statement balance to the corrected cash book balance. Bank charges (C) and dishonoured cheques (E) would appear on the bank statement and would have to be corrected in the cash book before reconciliation.

**34 A,C** Unpresented cheques, bank errors and uncredited lodgements are included in the reconciliation of the bank statement balance to the corrected cash book balance. Bank charges (C) and dishonoured cheques (A) would appear on the bank statement and would have to be corrected in the cash book before reconciliation.

**35 A,E,F**

Bank charges, direct debits and dishonoured cheques will all be written into the cash book. The other items affect the balance per the bank statement only.

**36 A** The correct entry is to debit payables control with the contra of £420 and irrecoverable debts expense with £240, then credit receivables control with the total £660

**37 B**

### BALANCES EXTRACTED FROM THE RECEIVABLES LEDGER

| | | + £ | – £ | £ |
|---|---|---|---|---|
| Total before corrections for errors | | | | 15,800 |
| Error (1) | Mahmood | 90 | | |
| Error (2) | Yasmin | 780 | | |
| Error (4) | Charles | | 200 | |
| Error (5) | Edward | 150 | | |
| | | 1,020 | 200 | 820 |
| | | | | 16,620 |

**38 B** This would be to treat it as revenue rather than capital expenditure

**39 A**

| | Cash book £ | Bank statement £ |
|---|---|---|
| | (27) | 625 |
| Unpresented cheques | | (327) |
| Direct debits | (200) | |
| Automated receipt | 525 | |
| | 298 | 298 |

**40 A** In preparing a bank reconciliation, uncredited lodgements reduce an overdrawn balance in the bank statement. If a cheque received from a customer is dishonoured after date, a credit entry in the cash book is required to reinstate the debt. Not all differences between the cash book and the bank statement must be corrected by means of a journal entry, since some items appear in the bank reconciliation only (eg errors by the bank, unpresented cheques and uncredited lodgements). Bank charges not yet entered in the cash book should be dealt with by updating the cash book, not by making an adjustment to the balance per the bank statement.

**41 A**

### SUSPENSE ACCOUNT

| | £ | | £ |
|---|---|---|---|
| Gas bill (420 – 240) | 180 | Interest receivable | 70 |
| Discount (50 x 2) | 100 | Balance c/d | 210 |
| | 280 | | 280 |
| Balance b/d (to be corrected) | 210 | | |

**42 A**

### PAYABLES CONTROL ACCOUNT

| | £ | | £ |
|---|---|---|---|
| Cash paid to suppliers | 988,400 | Opening balance | 384,600 |
| Discounts received | 12,600 | Purchases | 945,800 |
| Contras | 4,200 | | |
| Closing balance | 325,200 | | |
| | 1,330,400 | | 1,330,400 |

**43 B**

| | £ |
|---|---|
| Overdraft per bank statement | 39,800 |
| Less: deposits credited | (64,100) |
| Add: outstanding cheques | 44,200 |
| Overdraft per cash book | 19,900 |

**44 C** A transaction has been posted to the wrong account, but not the wrong class of account.

**45 C** (£3,204 + 780 – 370). The bank charges of £46 have already been charged by the bank, and so no further adjustment is required in relation to them.

**46 B** Transposition error in posting to the receivables ledger from the sales day book (B). In (A) and (C) both the ledger and the control account will be affected. In (D) only the control account would be affected.

**47 C** Balance omitted from the receivables ledger listing (C). Both would be affected by (B); in (A) and (D) the receivables ledger would be reduced.

**48 A** Dr suspense £2,840, Cr Discount received £2,840

**49 B** False – this is a control account posting therefore does not affect the individual balances in the ledger.
**C** True – the customer would overpay if it ignored a credit note.

**50 C** Debit Sales £230, Debit VAT control £46, Credit Receivables control £276

**51 B** A, C and D would make the supplier's statement £150 *higher*

**52 A** An expense has been posted as a non-current asset when it should have been a deduction from profit, non-current assets are overstated as a result.

**53 D** £807 should have been credited to payables, but instead it was debited to payables. Both the control account and the memorandum ledger should be credited with £807, to correct the error, and £807 again to record the invoice, ie increase both by (2 x £807) = £1,614

54 B Irina's discount needs to be debited to her payables ledger account (reducing it by £49) and credited to the control account to correct the duplicated debit (increasing the control account by £49).

55 D The trial balance is used as the starting point for producing an income statement and statement of financial position (D) when the ETB technique is being used, even if the final adjustments and corrections have not yet been put through. Even if the trial balance balances (A) there may still be compensating errors, and errors of commission and of principle in the ledger accounts. The trial balance lists out all the balances on the ledger accounts; it is not part of the ledger itself (B). When there is a credit balance on a suspense account this means that the total of debit balances initially exceeded the total of the credit balances (C).

SAMPLE PAPER

56 A,C Discount received should have been credited to an income statement account and debited to payables. Since both sides of the entry were debits, the debit side of the trial balance would exceed the credit side and a suspense account with a credit balance would be opened (A). Goods returned by a customer should have been debited to sales and credited to receivables. As they were debited to receivables the same situation arises, and a suspense account with a credit balance would be opened (C).

SAMPLE PAPER

57 B,C As some items have been drawn out by the owner rather than sold or carried forward as inventory, the purchases figure in cost of sales should be reduced or credited (B). A lower cost of sales figure means an increased reported profit (C).

SAMPLE PAPER

58 D This question is not asking for the balance on the suspense account, but for the adjustment made to the suspense account by the correcting journal.

A single journal to correct all these errors would be:

|  | £ | £ |
|---|---|---|
| CR Receivables (90 + 66) |  | 156 |
| DR Sales | 110 |  |
| DR Suspense (9,980 – 9,890) + (2 × 33) – 110 | 46 |  |
|  | 156 | 156 |

The debit entry in the suspense account is £46 (D)

SAMPLE PAPER

59 C The transposition error is £17,150 – £11,750 = £5,400. As the understatement is in the purchase day book total it affects only the control account, which is understated by £5,400 and so should be increased by that amount.

SAMPLE PAPER

60 B An overcast of the total of invoices in the sales day book means that £782 will be debited to the control account but not to the receivables ledger. In both A and C the receivables ledger will be overdebited by (£391 x 2); in D both the control account and the ledger will be overdebited by (391 x 2)

SAMPLE PAPER

61 A Employer's NIC is an expense to the business in addition to gross pay, so it should be debited to the salaries expense account from the control account (A). B is incorrect as it suggests that the *debit* balance on the control account should be *credited* to the liability account. Employees' NIC and PAYE are not additional expenses, so the remaining debit balance after gross pay has been charged cannot be these (C and D).

SAMPLE PAPER

**62 C** The difference in the amount at which the purchase of stamps was recorded is £120 – £12 = £108. As only £12 was recorded expenses have clearly been understated. Petty cash should have been topped up with (£36 + £60 + £120) = £216, so the £108 top-up is £216 – £108 = £108 too little (C).

**63 A** If the debit side of the trial balance is undercast by £692 this amount is debited in the suspense account. When the cheque payment of £905 was credited to cash it should have been debited to an expense account; instead it was debited to suspense. Thus the suspense account has a debit balance of £692 + £905 = £1,597

**64 D**

|  | £ |
|---|---|
| Uncorrected cash book balance | 42,510 |
| Dishonoured cheque | (2,470) |
| Corrected cash book balance | 40,040 |
| Unpresented cheques | 2,990 |
| Uncleared lodgements | (10,270) |
| Bank statement balance | 32,760 |

**65 A**

SUPPLIER ACCOUNT: ROCHELLE

|  | £ |  | £ |
|---|---|---|---|
| Cash (A) | 26 |  |  |

B, C     No effect yet on Rochelle's account

D  Paying £26 too little on an invoice would leave a credit balance on the account

**66 B** Item 2 is not an error; discounts allowed belong on the debit side of the trial balance.

SUSPENSE

|  | £ |  | £ |
|---|---|---|---|
| c/d | 2,512 | Item 1 (589 x 2) | 1,178 |
|  |  | Item 3 (667 x 2) | 1,334 |
|  | 2,512 |  | 2,512 |
|  |  | b/d | 2,512 (B) |

Option A includes items 1 and 2; Option C includes all three items; Option D includes items 2 and 3.

**67 A** When the cash receipt of £63 was recorded in receivables as £36, the entry was DR Cash £63, CR Receivables £36 and therefore CR Suspense £27 (A).

When the bad debt of £36 was recorded in receivables as £63, the entry was DR Bad debts expense £36, DR Suspense £27 and CR Receivables £63 (B).

When the sale to a credit customer of £63 was recorded in receivables as £36, the entry was DR Receivables £36, DR Suspense £27 and CR Sales £63 (C).

When the amount owed to a credit supplier of £63 was recorded in purchases as £36, the entry was DR Purchases £36, DR Suspense £27 and CR Payables £63 (D).

**68  A**  As opening inventory is a debit in the income statement, an overstatement or overvaluation here decreased profit and so should be added back. The reverse is true of closing inventory.

|  | £ |
|---|---|
| Draft gross profit | 99,500 |
| Add back: overstatement of opening inventory (3,720 x 25/125*) | 744 |
| Deduct: overstatement of closing inventory (1,240 x 25/125*) | (248) |
| Corrected gross profit | 99,996 (A) |

In Option B the overstatement in opening inventory is deducted, and that in closing inventory is added back. In the other two options the wrong gross profit percentage is applied, taking 25% margin (on sales value ie 25/100) rather than 25% mark-up (on cost).

* Gross profit percentages:

|  | % |
|---|---|
| Revenue | 125 |
| Cost | (100) |
| Gross profit | 25 |

To calculate gross profit from selling price, multiply by 25/125.

**69  B**  The whole of the subscription relates to the following year, so the instalment paid should all be treated as a prepayment, which reduces expenses in the year and so should be added back to the draft net profit.

The problem with the returned goods is that the draft net profit reflects the revenue made on sale of the goods, less the cost of those goods, therefore the profit on the sale should be deducted from the draft net profit.

|  | £ |
|---|---|
| Draft net profit | 75,000 |
| Add back: Prepaid subscription instalment (£1,000/2) | 500 |
| Deduct: profit on returned goods £400 x 75/25* | (1,200) |
|  | 74,300 (B) |

In A the profit deducted has been calculated as £400 x 25%; in C just the cost of goods (£400) has been deducted, while in D the profit has been added back and the prepayment deducted.

* Gross profit percentages:

|  | % |
|---|---|
| Revenue | 100 |
| Cost | (25) |
| Gross profit | 75 |

To calculate gross profit from cost, multiply by 75/25.

**70  A**  The repair costs should have been expensed fully to the income statement, reducing profits by £6,600, and the depreciation charged of £1,650 should be added back. The net effect is to decrease profits by £4,950.

In relation to the discount allowed, this should have been credited to trade receivables. There will however be no impact on profit when the error is corrected, as the correcting journal is

| CR | Trade receivables (1,785 x 2) |  | £3,570 |
|---|---|---|---|
| DR | Suspense | £3,570 |  |

|  | £ |
|---|---|
| Draft net profit | 540,000 |
| Net repair costs (6,600 x 0.75) | (4,950) |
| Clear suspense account | 0 |
| Final net profit | 535,050 (A) |

71  A  The absence of the missing inventory has already been reflected in the physical count, so effectively its cost has already been debited to gross profit, reducing both gross and net profit by £18,000. The insurance claim will be 40% x £18,000 = £7,200. This figure should be accounted for as follows:

DR   Other receivables          £7,200

CR   Other income                          £7,200

The credit entry increases net profit – NOT gross profit – by £7,200 (A).

72  D  If two credit notes for £484 each have been debited in the payables control account from the totals in the purchases day book, but only one has been debited direct to the payables ledger, then the payables ledger total will be £484 higher than the control account (D).

The effect of option A would be the ledger total being £484 lower than the control account, as the discount received has reduced the ledger but not the control account. The effect of option B would again be the control account being higher, as the overcast total would be posted to the control account but not to the ledger, where individual amounts are posted. The effect of option C is to reduce the payables ledger total by £484; the control account would be unaffected.

73  A, E  Recording a £30 contra (a credit entry) in the ledger only, and not in the control account, will cause the control account debit balance to be £30 higher than the ledger list (A). The cash book miscast of £15 will affect the control account only, as this is posted with the cash book total while the ledger is posted with individual entries from the cash book (E).

In options B and C neither the ledger nor the control account will be affected as there has been no record at all in a book of original entry. For option D both the ledger and the control account will be equally affected, as the information on the source document is incorrect but is accurately recorded in the book of original entry.

74  D  The interest credited of £126, added on the bank statement, has been correctly treated in the cash book already so no further adjustment is necessary.

|                             | £       |
|-----------------------------|---------|
| Original cash book balance  | 6,287   |
| Interest                    | 126     |
| Corrected cash book balance | 6,413   |
| Unpresented payments        | 2,113   |
| Uncredited lodgements       | (657)   |
| Balance per bank statement  | 7,869   |

75  B  A is incorrect because the error would arise in both the day book total (and would therefore be posted to the control account) and the list of payables ledger balances (which are derived from the individual day book entries).

B is correct because the payables ledger account of Zoinks plc will be understated by 2 x £730 = £1,460.

C is incorrect because although the payment to Scooby plc is posted to the incorrect payables ledger account, the entry is correctly on the debit side, and so the list of balances will equate to the control account.

D is incorrect because if the purchase day book is undercast, then the control account balance would be less than the list of balances.

76    B

1    Original entry DR Receivables control 120 CR Sales 120. Adjustment was just DR Sales 240 so a credit balance appears on suspense of £240. (Correction needed: CR Receivables control 240, DR Suspense 240.)

2    Should have DR Cash 75, CR Receivables control 75, but instead DR Cash 75, DR Payables control 75, so a credit balance appears on suspense of £150. (Correction needed: CR Receivables control 75, CR Payables control 75, DR Suspense 150.)

3    Should have DR Receivables control 455 CR Sales 455 but instead CR Receivables control 455 and CR Sales 455, so a debit balance appears on suspense of £910. (Correction needed: DR Receivables control 910 CR Suspense 910.)

### SUSPENSE

|  | £ |  | £ |
|---|---|---|---|
| b/d (bal fig) | 520 | Error 3 | 910 |
| Error 1 | 240 |  |  |
| Error 2 | 150 |  |  |
|  | 910 |  | 910 |

The figure of £640 in A and D would be arrived at if you ignored the fact that the bookkeeper rectified the sales account in full, removing the entry for £120 of invoices and then making the entry for £120 of credit notes.

77    C

|  | £ |
|---|---|
| Payables ledger balances at 31/12/X4 | 29,800 |
| Debit balance listed as credit balance (£153 x 2) | (306) |
| Corrected balance | 29,494 |
| Miscast of cash book (£2,950 – £2,590) | (360) |
| Original control account balance | 29,134 |

78    A

### CASH BOOK

|  | £ |  | £ |
|---|---|---|---|
| Direct credit | 8,642 | Balance b/d (bal fig) | 3,306 |
|  |  | Interest | 102 |
|  |  | c/d | 5,234 |
|  | 8,642 |  | 8,642 |

*Bank reconciliation statement*

|  | £ |
|---|---|
| Balance per bank statement (bal fig) | 6,600 |
| Add: Uncleared lodgements | 4,467 |
| Less: Unpresented cheques | (5,833) |
| Balance per cash book | 5,234 |

**79  C**  In A if the credit note is entered twice in the customer's account then the list of balances will be lower than the control account.

In B the error will arise in both the control account and the list of balances.

In D, the treatment of the cheque is correct in the control account, but the list of balances will understate the debt due from Vole plc. Therefore the control account total will be higher than the list of balances.

In C the receivables ledger will have been posted correctly but the control account will have been debited with £1,024 too little.

**80  D**

### RECEIVABLES LEDGER

|                          | £         |
| ------------------------ | --------- |
| Original balance         | 417,923   |
| Credit balance omitted (1) | (2,340)  |
| Corrected balance        | 415,583   |

### RECEIVABLES CONTROL ACCOUNT

|                              | £       |                                    | £       |
| ---------------------------- | ------- | ---------------------------------- | ------- |
| Original balance (bal fig)   | 418,265 | Irrecoverable debt (2)             | 882     |
|                              |         | SDB overstatement (3)              | 1,800   |
|                              |         | c/d (per receivables ledger)       | 415,583 |
|                              | 418,265 |                                    | 418,265 |

**81  D**  The rental income should have been credited to profit. The correcting journal is:

CR Profit (2,643 × 2)        £5,286

DR Suspense                            £5,286

If this is the case then profits will rise by £5,286, so the retained earnings figure will be:

|                          | £         |
| ------------------------ | --------- |
| Retained earnings b/d    | 860,610   |
| Profit after tax (draft) | 457,890   |
| Correcting journal       | 5,286     |
| Retained earnings c/d    | 1,323,786 |

**82  B**  The suspense account is increased by the imbalance in the adjustments processed (173 – 144) = 29:

|             | Initial TB | | Adjustments | | Revised TB | |
| ----------- | --- | --- | --- | --- | --- | --- |
|             | DR  | CR  | DR  | CR  | DR  | CR  |
|             | £   | £   | £   | £   | £   | £   |
| Suspense    | 78  |     | 29  |     | 107 |     |
| Adjustments |     |     | 144 | 173 |     |     |
| Total       |     |     | 173 | 173 |     |     |

**83  A**

1    The company DR Cash 1,509, CR Receivables 1,509 when it should have DR Cash 1,095, CR Receivables 1,095. To correct this it needs to remove (1,509 – 1,095) = 414 from each account:

DR Receivables 414, CR Cash 414

2    The company DR Payables 889, CR Cash 89 and therefore CR Suspense 800. To correct this it needs to reverse (889 – 89) = 800 from suspense to payables:

DR Suspense 800, CR Payables 800

Combined journal:

DR Suspense £800, DR Receivables £414, CR Payables £800, CR Cash £414 (A)

**84  B**    Discount allowed of £2,220 should have been debited to administrative expenses and credited to the receivables control account, so the payables control account needs to have the £2,220 reversed.

PAYABLES CONTROL ACCOUNT

|  | £ |  | £ |
|---|---|---|---|
| 1 Contra | 85 | b/d | 72,560 |
| c/d (bal fig) | 74,695 | 2 Admin expenses | 2,220 |
|  | 74,780 |  | 74,780 |

**85  D**    Discount allowed of £2,220 should have been debited to administrative expenses, not credited, so the adjustment to this account is a debit of £4,440 – the credits being £2,220 to the payables control account (wrongly debited before) and £2,220 to the receivables control account.

ADMINISTRATIVE EXPENSES

|  | £ |  | £ |
|---|---|---|---|
| b/d | 31,990 | Income statement (bal fig) | 36,430 |
| 2 PCA/RCA | 4,440 |  |  |
|  | 36,430 |  | 36,430 |

**86  B**    The incorrect entry was DR Prepayments £738, CR Suspense £738. Reversing this has no effect on profit. Making the correct entry of DR Expenses £738, CR Accruals £738 decreases profit by £738: £58,147 – £738 = £57,409 (B).

1    A    Income statement (8/12 x 60,000) + (4/12 x 48,000)

           Statement of financial position (2/12 x 60,000)

2    A    (2/3 × 798.00) + 898.80 + 814.80 + 840.00 + (1/3 × 966.00)

3    D

### RENT RECEIVABLE

| | £ | | £ |
|---|---|---|---|
| B/d arrears | 21,200 | B/d advances | 28,700 |
| Income statement (bal fig) | 475,900 | Cash received | 481,200 |
| C/d advances | 31,200 | C/d arrears | 18,400 |
| | 528,300 | | 528,300 |

4    B    £960 has been deducted from instead of added to profit. Therefore to cancel the error, you have to add it back then to post the correct entry you have to add it on again.

5    D

### SUBSCRIPTION INCOME ACCOUNT

| | £ | | £ |
|---|---|---|---|
| B/d arrears | 16,900 | B/d advances | 24,600 |
| Subscription income (bal fig) | 316,200 | Cash received | 318,600 |
| C/d advances | 28,400 | C/d arrears | 18,300 |
| | 361,500 | | 361,500 |

6    C

| | £ |
|---|---|
| Receipt | |
| 1 October 20X1 (£7,500 × 1/3) | 2,500 |
| 30 December 20X1 | 7,500 |
| 4 April 20X2 | 9,000 |
| 1 July 20X2 | 9,000 |
| 1 October 20X2 (£9,000 × 2/3) | 6,000 |
| Credit to income statement | 34,000 |
| | |
| Credit deferred income (£9,000 × 1/3) | 3,000 |

7    A    Income statement = £60,000 × 12/18 = £40,000

           Statement of financial position = £60,000 × 3/18 prepayment = £10,000

8    B    Income statement (8/12 x 90,000) + (4/12 x 120,000) = 100,000

           Statement of financial position 12,000/12 = 10,000

9    D

### RENTAL INCOME

| | £ | | £ |
|---|---|---|---|
| B/d arrears | 4,800 | B/d advances | 134,600 |
| Rental income (bal fig) | 828,700 | Cash received | 834,600 |
| C/d advances | 144,400 | C/d arrears | 8,700 |
| | 977,900 | | 977,900 |

**10 B**

| | £ |
|---|---|
| Income statement | |
| December to June 8,400 × 7/12 | 4,900 |
| July to November 12,000 × 5/12 | 5,000 |
| | 9,900 |

Other payables 12,000 × 1/12 = 1,000 (December rent received in advance)

**11 C**

| | £ |
|---|---|
| August to September 60,000 × 2/12 | 10,000 |
| October to July 72,000 × 10/12 | 60,000 |
| | 70,000 |

**12 C**

| | Income statement £ | Statement of financial position £ |
|---|---|---|
| Prepaid insurance | 8,200 | |
| Payment January 20X5 | 38,000 | |
| Prepayment July-Sept 20X5 | (9,500) | 9,500 |
| | 36,700 | 9,500 |

**13 A**

RENT RECEIVABLE

| | £ | | £ |
|---|---|---|---|
| B/d arrears | 3,800 | B/d advances | 2,400 |
| Income statement (bal fig) | 84,000 | Cash received | 83,700 |
| C/d advances | 3,000 | C/d arrears | 4,700 |
| | 90,800 | | 90,800 |

**14 A** Income statement $= (9/12 \times £10,800) + (3/12 \times £12,000) = £11,100$

Statement of financial position $=$ prepayment of $(9/12 \times £12,000)$

$= £9,000$

**15 B** 100,000 × 12% × 9/12 = £9,000 is payable (I/S), but only £6,000 has been paid (April and July).

**16 D** Income statement (5/12 x 24,000) + (7/12 x 30,000) = £27,500

Statement of financial position (2/12 x 30,000) = £5,000

**17 B**

ELECTRICITY ACCOUNT

| | | £ | | | £ |
|---|---|---|---|---|---|
| 20X0 | | | 20X0 | | |
| 1 August | Cash | 600 | 1 July | Accrual reversed | 300 |
| 1 November | Cash | 720 | | | |
| 20X1 | | | | | |
| 1 February | Cash | 900 | | | |
| 30 June | Cash | 840 | 20X1 | | |
| 30 June | Accrual £840 × 2/3 | 560 | 30 June | Income statement | 3,320 |
| | | 3,620 | | | 3,620 |

18   B   The total of the invoices

### GAS SUPPLIER PAYABLES ACCOUNT

|  |  | £ |  |  |  | £ |
|---|---|---|---|---|---|---|
| Balance b/d |  | 200 |  |  |  |  |
| Cash £600 x 12 |  | 7,200 | 28 February | Invoice |  | 1,300 |
|  |  |  | 31 May | Invoice |  | 1,400 |
|  |  |  | 31 August | Invoice |  | 2,100 |
|  |  |  | 30 November | Invoice |  | 2,000 |
|  |  |  | 30 November | Bal c/d |  | 600 |
|  |  | 7,400 |  |  |  | 7,400 |

19   D   £250 (reversed prepayment) + £800 (cash) + £90 accrual = £1,140

20   A   4,000 – 300 – (1,200/3)

21   B

### INSURANCE

|  | £ |  | £ |
|---|---|---|---|
| Reverse prepayment (bal fig) | 260 | Income statement | 1,760 |
| Cash | 1,820 | Prepayment | 320 |
|  | 2,080 |  | 2,080 |

22   B   (6/12 x (13,200 x 100/110)) + (6/12 x 13,200) = £12,600

23   D   Overstated by £800

24   B   £22,240 current asset

|  |  |  |
|---|---|---|
| Loan 12,000 + (12,000 x 2%) | = | £12,240 current asset |
| Insurance 9,000 x 8/12 | = | £6,000 current asset |
| Rent | = | £4,000 current asset |

25   C

|  | £ |
|---|---|
| 3/12 x (2,860 x 100/110) | 650 |
| 9/12 x £2,860 | 2,145 |
|  | 2,795 |

26   B

|  | £ |
|---|---|
| Opening inventory | 7,200 |
| Purchases | 76,500 |
| Carriage inwards | 50 |
| Less: closing inventory | (8,100) |
|  | 75,650 |

27   A   Debit electricity

     D   Credit insurance

     F   Credit accruals

     G   Debit prepayments

28   C   (£3,420 – 215 + 310) = £3,515

29   B   (£10,400 + 800 – 920) = £10,280

30   B, F   £60 has been prepaid as at the year end of 31 August 20X4, so this should be debited to the prepayments account (B) and credited to the telephone charges account (F).

31　C, F　Unpaid sales commission of £1,755 is an accrued expense which should be credited to accruals (F). As sales commission is a distribution cost it should be debited to this account (C).

SAMPLE PAPER

32　D　The prepayment of local property tax is for July and August, that is 2/3 x £6,495 = £4,330. This is debited to prepayments and credited to administrative expenses.

33　C　The closing prepayment should have been reversed to the debit side of the administrative expenses account in the new period. Entering it as a reversed accrual means that it has been credited. The account therefore needs to be debited with £215 to correct the error, and debited again to record the prepayment correctly – a total debit of £430

34　B　The opening prepayment of rent of £4,251 needs to be debited to administrative expenses, and the closing prepayment of £7,200 x 2/3 = £4,800 needs to be credited. Total administrative expenses will therefore be £44,064 + £4,251 – £4,800 = £43,515

SAMPLE PAPER

35　A　Cost of sales is £18,081 + £686,880 – £18,647 = £686,314

SAMPLE PAPER

36　B　Cost of sales includes carriage inwards, which is a cost incurred in bringing inventories to their present location, but excludes carriage outwards, which is a distribution cost and included in the income statement after calculating gross profit. Closing inventories should be deducted in arriving at cost of sales.

|  | £ |
|---|---|
| Purchases | 455,000 |
| Carriage inwards | 24,000 |
| Closing inventories | (52,000) |
| Cost of sales | 427,000 |

SAMPLE PAPER

37　A

RENT

|  | £ |  | £ |
|---|---|---|---|
| Advances | 7,720 | Receipts | 22,850 |
| Income statement (bal fig) | 19,620 | Arrears | 4,490 |
|  | 27,340 |  | 27,340 |

SAMPLE PAPER

38　A, C, D

Five months of the subscription has been prepaid at 31 August 20X8:

£240 x 5/12 = prepayment £100 (C)

Deposits of £75 will be treated as income in the subsequent year, so this must all be treated as deferred income £75 (A).

Five of the six months property tax relates to the year ended 31 August 20X8, so this must be accrued:

£5,400 x 5/6 = accrual £4,500 (D)

39　A, F　The company debited the cash book with the 20X3 rent received and credited rental income for 20X4, when it should have credited the rent receivable or accrued income asset account set up at 31 December 20X3. The correcting journal should therefore Debit Rental income (A) and Credit Accrued income (F).

**40 A** The bookkeeper has processed the opening (1) and closing (2) journals as follows:

### ACCRUALS

| | £ | | £ |
|---|---|---|---|
| | | b/d | 5,019 |
| | | Jnl 1 | 5,019 |
| | | Jnl 2 | 4,423 |

### PREPAYMENTS

| | £ | | £ |
|---|---|---|---|
| b/d | 2,816 | | |
| Jnl 1 | 2,816 | | |
| Jnl 2 | 3,324 | | |

### DISTRIBUTION COSTS

| | £ | | £ |
|---|---|---|---|
| Jnl 1 | 2,203 | Jnl 2 | 3,324 |
| Cash | 147,049 | | |
| Jnl 2 | 4,423 | | |

The cash payment and Journal 2 are correct. To correct Journal 1 the bookkeeper should:

Debit Accruals £10,038, Credit Prepayments £5,632, Credit Distribution costs £4,406

**41 B, F** Unless told otherwise we can assume that all charges accrue evenly in the period.

The Internet server charge payment of £4,500 made on 1 November 20X5 covers the six months to 30 April 20X6. Of this payment, four months is a prepayment covering the period 1 January to 30 April 20X6, an amount of (4/6 x £4,500) = £3,000 (B).

The telephone rental payments are in arrears, so when the last payment for 20X5 is made on 30 November, Bez plc still owes one month (December) of rental, which is (£7,440 x 1/12) = £620 (F).

**42 B** Having paid its 20X4/X5 fee in advance, Butters plc is now paying its 20X5/X6 fee in arrears. The amount unpaid at 30 June 20X5 will therefore be an accrual. There are outstanding fees for the period 1 March-30 June 20X5, which is four months. The accrual is therefore £21,000 x 1.125 x 4/12 = £7,875 (B).

# Chapter 8: Irrecoverable debts and allowances

1    B    Debit irrecoverable debts expense, credit receivables control

2    A    1,300 + 2,150 − (8,540 − 6,631) = £1,541

3    B    False

     C    True: irrecoverable debts expense hits net profit not gross profit

4    C

|  | £ |
|---|---|
| Balance per trial balance | 50,000 |
| Less bad debt written off | (3,250) |
| Less cash received from T Ruin | (1,700) |
|  | 45,050 |

Adjustment (2) will be to the allowance, not to receivables; adjustment (3) affects irrecoverable debts

5    D    (28,500 + (42,000 − 38,000))

6    D    £1,005 credit

|  | £ |
|---|---|
| Specific allowance | 495 |
| b/f allowance | 1,000 |
| Reduction (credit) | 505 |
| Bad debt recovered (credit) | 500 |
|  | 1,005 |

7    C

|  | £ |
|---|---|
| Specific allowance | 2,157 |
| Opening allowance | 2,050 |
| Increase in allowance | 107 |
| Irrecoverable debts | 985 |
|  | 1,092 |

8    C

### IRRECOVERABLE DEBTS EXPENSE

|  | £ |  | £ |
|---|---|---|---|
| Write off | 280 | Decrease in allowance (1,000 −100) | 900 |
| Income statement (bal fig) | 1,120 | Cash | 500 |
|  | 1,400 |  | 1,400 |

9    D

|  | £ |
|---|---|
| Closing allowance required | 36,200 |
| Opening allowance | 50,000 |
| Decrease in allowance | (13,800) |
| Irrecoverable debts written off | 38,000 |
| Income statement charge | 24,200 |

**10  A**

| | £ |
|---|---:|
| Irrecoverable debts written off | 14,600 |
| Reduction in allowance (18,000 – 16,000) | (2,000) |
| | 12,600 |

**11  A**

### RECEIVABLES

| | £ | | £ |
|---|---:|---|---:|
| B/d debit balances | 32,750 | B/d credit balances | 1,275 |
| Sales | 125,000 | Cash | 122,500 |
| Refunds | 1,300 | Discounts | 550 |
| | | C/d | 34,725 |
| | 159,050 | | 159,050 |

**12  C**  (800 × 0.6) + 2,965 = £3,445

**13  C**

### RECEIVABLES CONTROL ACCOUNT

| | £ | | £ |
|---|---:|---|---:|
| Opening balance | 284,680 | Cash received | 179,790 |
| Credit sales | 194,040 | Discounts allowed | 3,660 |
| | | Irrecoverable debts written off | 1,800 |
| | | Additional write-off | 4,920 |
| | | Contras | 800 |
| | | Closing balance | 287,750 |
| | 478,720 | | 478,720 |

**14  B**

| | £ |
|---|---:|
| Allowance for receivables | 24,000 |
| Previous allowance | (39,000) |
| Reduction | (15,000) |
| Debts written off | 37,000 |
| Charge to income statement | 22,000 |

**15  B**

| | £ |
|---|---:|
| Allowance required | 21,500 |
| Existing allowance | (18,000) |
| Increase required | 3,500 |
| | |
| Charge to income statement (28,000 + 3,500) | 31,500 |

**16  B**  Trade receivables  = £838,000 – £72,000

= £766,000

Allowance for receivables is increased by £12,000 to £60,000

17 C

|  | £ |
|---|---|
| Closing receivables allowance | 22,575 |
| Deduct opening balance | (22,000) |
| Additional allowance | 575 |
| Add write off | 27,500 |
| Total charge | 28,075 |

18 D Net profit increases by £300

19 B

|  | £ |
|---|---|
| Allowance required | 42,550 |
| Existing allowance | (48,000) |
| Reduction in allowance | (5,450) |
| Irrecoverable debts written off | 13,000 |
| Income statement charge | 7,550 |

Net receivables = £864,000 – 13,000 – 42,550

= £808,450

20 C a debit entry of £4,055 to irrecoverable debt expense

D a credit entry of £2,400 to trade receivables

E a credit entry of £1,655 to allowance for receivables

21 A, B, F

Neither an increase in the allowance nor discounts received affect receivables control

RECEIVABLES CONTROL

|  | £ |  | £ |
|---|---|---|---|
| Sales (E) | X | Cash received (A) | X |
| Refunds (G) | X | Irrecoverable debts (B) | X |
|  |  | Credit notes (F) | X |
|  | X |  | X |

22 A The balancing figure in the allowance account will be a debit in the income statement

ALLOWANCE FOR RECEIVABLES

|  | £ |  | £ |
|---|---|---|---|
| Carried down | 3,600 | Brought down | 3,000 |
|  |  | Income statement (bal fig) | 600 |
|  | 3,600 |  | 3,600 |

23 C An allowance of £10,380 x 0.75 = £7,785 is needed (C). The charge will be £7,785 – £500 + £508 = £7,793 (C)

**24  A, B, F**

The allowance needs to be debited with £6,546 – £5,060 = £1,486 (B), and £1,860 needs to be credited to trade receivables (F). The net debit to the irrecoverable debt expense account is therefore £1,860 – £1,486 = £374 (A)

### ALLOWANCE FOR RECEIVABLES

| | £ | | £ |
|---|---|---|---|
| Carried down (£12,650 x 0.4) | 5,060 | Brought down | 6,546 |
| Irrecoverable debts expense (B) | 1,486 | | |
| | 6,546 | | 6,546 |

### IRRECOVERABLE DEBT EXPENSE

| | £ | | £ |
|---|---|---|---|
| Trade receivables | 1,860 | Allowance decreased | 1,486 |
| | | Income statement | 374 |
| | 1,860 | | 1,860 |

SAMPLE PAPER

**25  A**  Using T accounts for the allowance and the charge, we can see that the charge is £2,251 (A) and the figure for receivables is £578,645 – £250 = £578,395 (A)

### ALLOWANCE FOR RECEIVABLES

| | £ | | £ |
|---|---|---|---|
| C/d | 250 | B/d | 1,200 |
| Irrecoverable debts | 950 | | |
| | 1,200 | | 1,200 |

### IRRECOVERABLE DEBT EXPENSE

| | £ | | £ |
|---|---|---|---|
| Draft charge | 3,290 | Allowance | 950 |
| | | Recovered debt | 89 |
| | | Income statement | 2,251 |
| | 3,290 | | 3,290 |

SAMPLE PAPER

**26  D**  For (3), the entry made was DR Cash £58, CR Suspense £58; the suspense account entry must be reversed to the credit of the irrecoverable debts expense account.

### SUSPENSE

| | £ | | £ |
|---|---|---|---|
| Correct 3 | 58 | b/d | 58 |
| | 58 | | 58 |

### ALLOWANCE FOR IRRECOVERABLE DEBTS

| | £ | | £ |
|---|---|---|---|
| 2 Decrease in allowance (bal fig) | 25 | b/d | 500 |
| c/d | 475 | | |
| | 500 | | 500 |

### IRRECOVERABLE DEBTS EXPENSE

| | £ | | £ |
|---|---|---|---|
| Write off debt | 92 | 2 Reduce allowance | 25 |
| | | Correct 3 | 58 |

The net debit to the irrecoverable debt account is therefore (92 – 25 – 58) = £9.

### CASH

| | £ | | £ |
|---|---|---|---|
| | | Record returned cheque | 92 |

### ALLOWANCE FOR RECEIVABLES

|  | £ |  | £ |
|---|---|---|---|
| c/d Ost plc (950 – 500) | 450 | b/d Basnet plc | 1,425 |
| Irrecoverable debts (bal fig) | 1,925 | b/d Ost plc | 950 |
|  | 2,375 |  | 2,375 |

### IRRECOVERABLE DEBTS EXPENSE

|  | £ |  | £ |
|---|---|---|---|
| Basnet plc (1,425 – 200) | 1,225 | Allowance for receivables | 1,925 |
| Administrative expenses (bal fig) | 700 |  |  |
|  | 1,925 |  | 1,925 |

In the administrative expenses account the amount for irrecoverable debts will be a credit of £700.

1   A   Closing inventory = 200 + 1,000 + 800 + 300 − 700 − 400 − 500 = 700 units

|  |  | £ |
|---|---|---|
| FIFO | 400 @ 6.20 | 2,480 |
|  | 300 @ 6.60 | 1,980 |
|  | 700 | 4,460 |

2   C   In this example, cost includes both direct materials/labour and also production overheads.

NRV is expected selling price less expected selling costs.

|  | Cost £ | NRV £ | Lower of cost/NRV £ |
|---|---|---|---|
| Category 1 | 4,570 | 5,320 | 4,570 |
| Category 2 | 12,090 | 11,890 | 11,890 |
| Category 3 | 2,300 | 2,370 | 2,300 |
|  | 18,960 | 19,580 | 18,760 |

3   C

|  |  | £ |
|---|---|---|
| Product A | 5,500 × £10 = | 55,000 |
|  | 500 × £8 = | 4,000 |
| Product B | 1,900 × £5 = | 9,500 |
|  | 100 × £3 = | 300 |
|  |  | 68,800 |

4   B   False: if prices are rising, the charge to cost of sales will be higher if AVCO is used. Gross profit will therefore be lower under this method.

      D   False: closing inventory is a debit in the statement of financial position and a credit in the income statement.

5   A

|  | Units | Cost(£) | Av cost(£) | Value(£) |
|---|---|---|---|---|
| 1.6.X8 | 60 | 12 |  | 720 |
| 8.6.X8 | 40 | 15 |  | 600 |
| 14.6.X8 | 50 | 18 |  | 900 |
|  | 150 |  | 14.80 | 2,220 |
| 21.6.X8 | (75) |  | 14.80 | (1,110) |
|  | 75 |  |  | 1,110 |

6   B

|  | £ |
|---|---|
| Cost | 46 |
| Production overheads | 15 |
|  | 61 |

|  | £ |
|---|---|
| Net realisable value |  |
| Sales price | 80 |
| Less modification costs | (17) |
| Less selling costs (80 × 10%) | (8) |
|  | 55 |

7   B   False – it is current asset inventory.

      C   True – import duties should be included in inventory cost.

8   A, E  (B), (C) and (D) are distribution costs.

9    D    Regarding (A), LIFO is not an acceptable inventory valuation method. Overheads may be included in cost (B), and replacement cost is not considered when identifying the lower of cost and NRV (C).

10    A

| | £ |
|---|---|
| Original value | 284,700 |
| Coats – Cost 400 × £80 | (32,000) |
|       – NRV (£75 × 95%) × 400 | 28,500 |
| | 281,200 |

At 31 January 20X3 the skirts were correctly valued at costs incurred to date of £20 per skirt which was lower than the NRV of £22. Therefore no adjustment required.

11    B

| | Cost | Net realisable value | Lower of cost & NRV | Units | Value |
|---|---|---|---|---|---|
| | £ | £ | £ | | £ |
| Basic | 6 | 8 | 6 | 200 | 1,200 |
| Super | 9 | 8 | 8 | 250 | 2,000 |
| Luxury | 18 | 10 | 10 | 150 | 1,500 |
| | | | | | 4,700 |

12    A

| | £ |
|---|---|
| 50 @ £190 | 9,500 |
| 500 @ £220 | 110,000 |
| 300 @ £230 | 69,000 |
| | 188,500 |

13    D    (10 units x £45) + (50 units x £50) = £2,950

14    D

| | £ |
|---|---|
| Inventory check balance | 483,700 |
| Less: goods from suppliers | (38,400) |
| Add: goods sold | 14,800 |
| Less: goods returned | (400) |
| Add: goods returned to supplier | 1,800 |
| | 461,500 |

15    C    If closing inventory is understated, cost of sales will be overstated and profit will be understated. Next year's opening inventory will be understated and its cost of sales will be understated, so its profit will be overstated.

16    A

| | £ | £ |
|---|---|---|
| Original balance | | 386,400 |
| Item (1) Cost | (18,000) | |
| NRV 15,000 – 800 | 14,200 | |
| Write down | | (3,800) |
| Inventory value | | 382,600 |

17    A

| | £ |
|---|---|
| Inventory count value | 836,200 |
| Less: purchases | (8,600) |
| Add: sales (14,000 x 70/100) | 9,800 |
| Add: goods returned | 700 |
| Inventory figure | 838,100 |

18  A

|  | £ |  |
|---|---|---|
| B/d | 284,000 | |
| Item 1 | – | No change as NRV exceeds cost |
| Item 2 | (350) | Reduce to NRV (1,000 – 800 +150) |
| | 283,650 | |

19  C  (20 x £12.50) + (40 x £12.80) + (60 x £13.00) + (72 x £13.50) + (8 x £10) = £2,594

20  B  (20 x £5) + (20 x (£15 – 10 – 1)) = £180

21  C  £60,600

200 items × £15 = £3,000

NRV = (200 × £17.50) – 1,200 – 300 = £2,000

400 items = (400 × £1.50) – 200 = £400

Total = £58,200 + £2,000 + £400 = £60,600

22  A  $100 \times$ (£400 – £110 – £65) + (100 × £350) = £57,500

23  C  Cost can include both inward transport costs and production overheads.

24  B  A and C would not explain a shortfall and D is the correct treatment. B will cause cost of sales to be overstated and so reduce the mark-up.

25  A

|  | £'000 | £'000 | % |
|---|---|---|---|
| Sales | | 125 | 125 |
| Opening inventory | 35 | | |
| Purchases | 80 | | |
| Closing inventory (bal fig) | (15) | | |
| Cost of sales (125,000 × 100/125) | | 100 | 100 |
| Gross profit | | 25 | 25 |

26  B  £125,000 × 80% = £100,000

27  B  Options A and C would increase the gross profit margin. Option D would not affect gross profit.

28  C  19,200/96,000 × 100% = 20%

29  B, C  Income statement = credit    Statement of financial position = debit

30  C, G  The value of closing inventory is (£572,904 – £27,485 + £15,000) = £560,419. This should be debited and credited to the closing inventory account; the debit is for the statement of financial position and the credit is for the income statement

SAMPLE PAPER

31  A

| | | Units | Value | |
|---|---|---|---|---|
| | | | £ | £ |
| 8/X4 | b/f | 2,400 | 10.00 | 24,000 |
| 11/X4 | Sell | (900) | 10.00 | (9,000) |
| | | 1,500 | 10.00 | 15,000 |
| 1/X5 | Buy | 1,200 | 16.75 | 20,100 |
| | | 2,700 | 13.00 | 35,100 |
| 5/X5 | Sell | (1,800) | 13.00 | (23,400) |
| 7/X5 | c/f | 900 | 13.00 | 11,700 |

32  A   When raw material prices are rising, AVCO averages the earlier, lower prices with the later, higher prices, while FIFO just takes the later, higher prices. Thus FIFO would result in a higher inventory value than AVCO. As inventory quantities are constant, this means that closing inventory would always be higher than opening inventory. As closing inventory is a reduction in the cost of sales calculation, all other things being equal this would result in the overall debit balance of cost of sales being lower under FIFO than under AVCO: hence lower cost of sales and higher closing inventory value (A).

33  C   To calculate cost of sales correctly the purchases figure should only take into consideration the goods purchased for resale. Therefore it is necessary to reduce purchases, not inventory, by the cost of the inventory destroyed (CR Purchases £36,000). This cost to the business should be shown under administrative expenses in the income statement (DR Administrative expenses £36,000). The sum due from the insurance company of £28,800 should be treated as part of other income, not revenue, as it is from a non-trading source (CR Other income £28,800).

1   B   The cost of the machine is £28,000. Cataract has paid £23,000 in cash and has evidently
        agreed a trade-in value of £5,000 for the old machine. (The old asset's carrying amount is
        irrelevant.) After one year, the carrying amount of the new machine is 90% of £28,000 =
        £25,200.

2   C

|  | £ |
|---|---|
| Cost (15,000 + 1,300 + 2,500) | 18,800 |
| Depreciation (10% × 18,800) | (1,880) |
| Carrying amount | 16,920 |

3   B

|  | £ |
|---|---|
| Cost of asset | 22,000 |
| Accumulated depreciation (46 months × (21,000/84)) | (11,500) |
| Carrying amount at date of disposal | 10,500 |
| Proceeds on disposal | 9,000 |
| Loss on disposal | 1,500 |

4   A

### DISPOSAL

|  | £ |  | £ |
|---|---|---|---|
| Cost | 20,000 | Depreciation | 14,200 |
|  |  | Trade in allowance (22,000 – 17,500) | 4,500 |
|  |  | ∴ loss | 1,300 |
|  | 20,000 |  | 20,000 |

5   A   (6,000 – 300)/(5 × 12) = £95. This year 6 × £95 = £570

6   C   £23,500 × 90% = £21,150

7   A   £18,000 × 75% × 75% – 5,000 = £5,125 loss

8   D   To match the cost of the non-current asset with the revenue that the asset generates.

9   C   Any abnormal costs are not directly attributable to the asset and therefore should not be
        capitalised.

10  A   Purchased goodwill is retained in the statement of financial position subject to an impairment
        review.

11  D   (£5,000 – £1,000)/4 = £1,000 depreciation per annum for 3 years

### DISPOSAL

|  | £ |  | £ |
|---|---|---|---|
| Cost | 5,000 | Depreciation | 3,000 |
|  |  | Proceeds | 1,600 |
|  |  | ∴ loss | 400 |
|  | 5,000 |  | 5,000 |

**12 B**

| | | £ |
|---|---|---:|
| Cost | | 1,000,000 |
| 20X1 Depreciation | | 250,000 |
| | | 750,000 |
| 20X2 Depreciation | | 187,500 |
| | | 562,500 |
| 20X3 Depreciation | | 140,625 |
| | | 421,875 |
| 20X4 Part exchange | | 500,000 |
| Profit | | 78,125 |

**13 D**

| | £ |
|---|---:|
| Balance b/d | 67,460 |
| Less: Cost of non-current asset sold | (15,000) |
| Add: accumulated depreciation of asset sold (15,000 – (4,000 + 1,250)) | 9,750 |
| | 62,210 |

**14 A** If disposal proceeds were £15,000 and profit on disposal is £5,000, then carrying amount must be £10,000, the difference between the asset register figure and the non-current asset account in the nominal ledger.

**15 C** 48,000 + 400 + 2,200 = 50,600

**16 D**

| | £ |
|---|---:|
| December addition – 18,000 × 20% × 10/12 | 3,000 |
| June disposal – 36,000 × 20% × 8/12 | 4,800 |
| Balance – 345,200 × 20% | 69,040 |
| | 76,840 |

**17 A** (200,000 – 20,000 – 25,000 – 5,000 = 150,000)

**18 A**

| | | £ |
|---|---|---:|
| Plant held all year | (380,000 – 30,000) × 20% | 70,000 |
| New plant | (51,000 x 20% × 9/12) | 7,650 |
| Plant disposed of | (30,000 × 20% × 9/12) | 4,500 |
| | | 82,150 |

**19 A**

| | £ |
|---|---:|
| Plant held all year (200,000 – 40,000) × 20% | 32,000 |
| Disposal 40,000 × 20% × 9/12 | 6,000 |
| Additions 50,000 × 20% × 6/12 | 5,000 |
| | 43,000 |

**20 A** £36,000/120 x 3 = £900

**21 D**

The machine has had 3 years' depreciation at 40% reducing balance.

| | £ |
|---|---:|
| Carrying amount is therefore (£35,000 x 60% × 60% × 60%) = | 7,560 |
| Add profit on disposal | 2,440 |
| Part-exchange allowance | 10,000 |
| Payment | 30,000 |
| Price of new machine | 40,000 |

**22 A** £18,000 × 90% = £16,200

**23 A** (£10,000 × 70% × 70%) – £6,000 = £1,100

24  B  $(£120,000 - 4,000)/48 \times 3 = £7,250$

25  C

|  |  | £ |
|---|---|---|
| Draft net profit |  | 83,600 |
| Add: purchase price |  | 18,000 |
| Less: additional depreciation (18,000 × 25%) |  | (4,500) |
| Adjusted profit |  | 97,100 |

26  B  The internal administration costs cannot be treated as part of the asset's cost, so in the first two years' depreciation of (£96,720 + £3,660)/5 × 2 = £40,152 was charged. This means that the whole of the remaining carrying amount of £60,228 must be allocated as depreciation in 20X6 given the revision of the asset's useful life.

27  B, C  The error in the cost and accumulated depreciation nominal ledger accounts means that an asset with a carrying amount of (£351,080 – £300,070) = £51,010 must be credited to these accounts and debited to the disposal account. This is balanced in the disposal account by disposal proceeds of £40,950 and a loss on disposal of £10,060 both being credited (B), and also by disposal proceeds of £61,070 being credited and a profit on disposal of £10,060 being debited (C).

28  C  The initial amount capitalised is £44,500, as the licence cost is excluded from the value of the plant because it is not a directly attributable cost.

Depreciation is initially ((44,500 – 3,500)/8) = £5,125 per annum, so at 1 June 20X5 the carrying amount is (44,500 – (2 × 5,125)) = £34,250. Depreciation is then charged at 40% on this figure, giving a depreciation figure of £13,700 for the year to 31 May 20X6, and a carrying amount of £20,550.

PLANT – COST

|  | £ |  | £ |
|---|---|---|---|
| Purchase price | 43,000 | c/d | 44,500 |
| Transport | 1,500 |  |  |
|  | 44,500 |  | 44,500 |

PLANT – ACCUMULATED DEPRECIATION

|  | £ |  | £ |
|---|---|---|---|
| c/d | 23,950 | 31/5/X4 Charge (44,500 – 3,500)/8 | 5,125 |
|  |  | 31/5/X5 Charge (44,500 – 3,500)/8 | 5,125 |
|  |  | 31/5/X6 (44,500 – 10,250) x 0.4 | 13,700 |
|  | 23,950 |  | 23,950 |

Carrying amount: 44,500 – 23,950 = £20,550

29  C

DISPOSAL

|  | £ |  | £ |
|---|---|---|---|
| Cost | 23,500 | Accumulated depreciation £23,500 - (£23,500 x 0.7 x 0.7) | 11,985 |
|  |  | Part exchange value (£28,200 – £19,350) | 8,850 |
|  |  | Loss on disposal (bal fig) | 2,665 |
|  | 23,500 |  | 23,500 |

**30  C**   The debit to administrative expenses is the loss on disposal of £1,898

### DISPOSAL

| | £ | | £ |
|---|---|---|---|
| Cost | 4,000 | Acc dep (£4,000 – (£4,000 x 0.8 x 0.8 x 0.8)) | 1,952 |
| | | Proceeds | 150 |
| | | Administrative expenses (loss on disposal) | 1,898 |
| | 4,000 | | 4,000 |

**31  B**   This is calculated using T accounts, the carrying amount being £626,000 – £368,165 = £257,835. Note that no depreciation will be charged in the year to 31 March 20X6 for the asset acquired at the year end:

### COST

| | £ | | £ |
|---|---|---|---|
| B/d | 614,500 | | |
| Additions | 11,500 | C/d | 626,000 |
| | 626,000 | | 626,000 |

### ACCUMULATED DEPRECIATION

| | £ | | £ |
|---|---|---|---|
| | | B/d (614,500 – 399,960) | 214,540 |
| C/d | 368,165 | Charge (614,500 x 0.25) | 153,625 |
| | 368,165 | | 368,165 |

**32  B**   The incorrect figure of £196,800 is arrived at by using a single carrying amount T account and mixing up the b/d and c/d figures.

### FIXTURES & FITTINGS – COST

| | £ | | £ |
|---|---|---|---|
| b/d | 480,000 | Disposals – bal fig | 164,000 |
| Additions | 284,000 | c/d | 600,000 |
| | 764,000 | | 764,000 |

### FIXTURES & FITTINGS – ACCUMULATED DEPRECIATION

| | £ | | £ |
|---|---|---|---|
| Disposals – bal fig | 104,400 | b/d | 218,000 |
| c/d | 180,000 | Charge | 66,400 |
| | 284,400 | | 284,400 |

### DISPOSALS

| | £ | | £ |
|---|---|---|---|
| F&F – cost | 164,000 | F&F – acc dep | 104,400 |
| IS – Profit on disposal | 119,200 | Proceeds | 178,800 |
| | 283,200 | | 283,200 |

## 33 C

### PLANT & MACHINERY – COST

|  | £ |  | £ |
|---|---|---|---|
| b/d | 92,000 | Disposals – bal fig | 21,000 |
| Additions | 39,000 | c/d | 110,000 |
|  | 131,000 |  | 131,000 |

### PLANT & MACHINERY – ACCUMULATED DEPRECIATION

|  | £ |  | £ |
|---|---|---|---|
| Disposals – bal fig | 6,000 | b/d | 51,000 |
| c/d | 72,000 | Charge | 27,000 |
|  | 78,000 |  | 78,000 |

### DISPOSALS

|  | £ |  | £ |
|---|---|---|---|
| P&M – cost | 21,000 | P&M – acc dep | 6,000 |
|  |  | Proceeds – bal fig | 13,000 |
|  |  | Loss | 2,000 |
|  | 21,000 |  | 21,000 |

## 34 D

The accumulated depreciation at the part exchange date is (60,000 – 34,400) = £25,600, and this must be eliminated from the accumulated depreciation account by debiting the account.

The machine cost account is debited with the difference between the cost of the old and new machines (196,600 – 60,000) = £136,600

Anaconda is paying a total cash/payables figure of (110,000 + 42,000) = £152,000 for the machine, therefore the part-exchange allowance is (196,600 – 152,000) = £44,600. This is compared to the carrying amount of £34,400 to give a gain on disposal of £10,200

| DR | Accumulated depreciation | £25,600 |
|---|---|---|
| DR | Cost | £136,600 |
| CR | Disposal | £10,200 |
| CR | Suspense | £152,000 |

### MACHINE – COST

|  | £ |  | £ |
|---|---|---|---|
| Cash | 110,000 | Disposal | 60,000 |
| Trade and other payables | 42,000 | c/d | 136,600 |
| Part exchange value | 44,600 |  |  |
|  | 196,600 |  | 196,600 |
| b/d (net entry) | 136,600 |  |  |

### DISPOSAL

|  | £ |  | £ |
|---|---|---|---|
| Cost | 60,000 | Accumulated depreciation | 25,600 |
| c/d Profit on disposal | 10,200 | Part exchange value | 44,600 |
|  | 70,200 |  | 70,200 |
|  |  | b/d (net entry) | 10,200 |

## 35 D

VAT on vehicles except for cars is treated as input tax, so the truck's cost in the ledger accounts is £99,900 × 5/6 = £83,250 (B). This is depreciated at 20% per annum for 6 months, a charge of £8,325. Hence the carrying amount at the year end is £83,250 – £8,325 = £74,925 (D).

In option C the cost is depreciated for a full year (£83,250 × 0.8), while in A the cost is taken to include VAT, and is then depreciated for six months.

**36  D**  VAT is not treated as input tax when a car is purchased for use in a business (as opposed to being bought as inventory by a car dealer). As Crocker plc is a retailer we can assume that the gross figure should be taken as the cost of both vehicles. The old car had been depreciated for 28 months when it was traded in.

DISPOSALS

| | £ | | £ |
|---|---|---|---|
| Old car – cost | 16,800 | Vehicles – acc dep (16,800/60 x 28) | 7,840 |
| | | Part exchange value ((17,625 x 1.2) – 13,500) | 7,650 |
| | | Loss – bal fig | 1,310  (D) |
| | 16,800 | | 16,800 |

Note that in Option A the error is to have depreciated the old car for only two years, assuming a policy of 'full year's depreciation in the year of purchase and none in the year of sale'. In Option B the net price of the new car is used when calculating the part exchange value, while in Option C both these errors are made.

**37  B**  In respect of the disposal, the computer sold had a carrying amount of £6,800/4 × 2 = £3,400 at 1 January 20X4, so a loss of (3,400 – 1,800) = £1,600 arises on disposal.

The remaining computers have a cost of £997,608 (1,004,408 – 6,800). We know that none of them was written down fully at the previous year end, and we can assume there have been no additions, so depreciation of £997,608/4 = £249,402 arises.

ADMINISTRATIVE EXPENSES

| | £ | | £ |
|---|---|---|---|
| b/d | 684,000 | Income statement | 935,002 |
| Disposal | 1,600 | | |
| Depreciation charge | 249,402 | | |
| | 935,002 | | 935,002 |

COMPUTERS – COST

| | £ | | £ |
|---|---|---|---|
| b/d | 1,004,408 | Disposal | 6,800 |
| | | c/d | 997,608 |
| | 1,004,408 | | 1,004,408 |

COMPUTERS – ACCUMULATED DEPRECIATION

| | £ | | £ |
|---|---|---|---|
| Disposal (6,800/4 x 2) | 3,400 | b/d | 697,600 |
| c/d | 943,602 | Charge (997,608/4) | 249,402 |
| | 947,002 | | 947,002 |

DISPOSAL

| | £ | | £ |
|---|---|---|---|
| Cost | 6,800 | Accumulated depreciation | 3,400 |
| | | Proceeds | 1,800 |
| | | Loss (bal fig) | 1,600 |
| | 6,800 | | 6,800 |

ICAEW

38  D  Carrying amount of computer traded in = £24,000 × 60% × 60% = £8,640.

Carrying amount of remaining computers is therefore 150,000 + 34,600 – 8,640 = £175,960. Depreciation on these is (175,960 × 40%) = £70,384 (D).

COMPUTERS – CARRYING AMOUNT

|  | £ |  | £ |
|---|---|---|---|
| b/d | 150,000 | Disposal (24,000 x 0.6 x 0.6) | 8,640 |
| Additions | 34,600 | Charge (175,960 x 40%) | 70,384 |
|  |  | c/d | 105,576 |
|  | 184,600 |  | 184,600 |

1  A  20,000 × £0.25 = £5,000

2  A

3  B

### SHARE CAPITAL

|  | £m |  | £m |
|---|---|---|---|
|  |  | Bal b/d | 100 |
|  |  | Share premium (bonus) | 50 |
| Bal c/d | 210 | Cash (rights) | 60 |
|  | 210 |  | 210 |

### SHARE PREMIUM

|  | £m |  | £m |
|---|---|---|---|
| Share capital (bonus) | 50 | Bal b/d | 80 |
| Bal c/d | 60 | Cash (rights) | 30 |
|  | 110 |  | 110 |

4  B  Share capital will be credited with the nominal value of the shares (1m × 50p) – the balance goes to share premium (1m × 30p).

5  B  This is the transfer of the premium to the share premium account.

6  C  A bonus issue does not involve cash but can be financed from the share premium account.

7  B

|  | £ |
|---|---|
| Equity shares at start of year | 50,000 |
| Add: bonus issue 50,000 × 50p | 25,000 |
| Add: new issue 60,000 × 50p | 30,000 |
|  | 105,000 |
|  |  |
| Share premium at start of year | 180,000 |
| Less: bonus issue 50,000 × 50p | (25,000) |
| Add: new issue 60,000 × 30p | 18,000 |
|  | 173,000 |

8  A

|  | £ |
|---|---|
| Debit cash | 1,100,000 |
| Credit share capital | 250,000 |
| Credit share premium | 850,000 |

9  B  False

   D  False. Extraordinary items are prohibited. Dividends appear in the retained earnings account not the income statement.

**10   B**

### SHARE CAPITAL

|  | Number | £ |  | Number | £ |
|---|---|---|---|---|---|
|  |  |  | Bal b/d | 500,000 | 125,000 |
|  |  |  | 1 for 2 rights | 250,000 | 62,500 |
|  |  |  |  | 750,000 |  |
| Bal c/d | 900,000 | 225,000 | 1 for 5 bonus | 150,000 | 37,500 |
|  | 900,000 | 225,000 |  | 900,000 | 225,000 |

### SHARE PREMIUM

|  | £ |  | £ |
|---|---|---|---|
| 1 for 5 bonus | 37,500 | Bal b/d | 100,000 |
| Bal c/d | 250,000 | 1 for 2 rights | 187,500 |
|  | 287,500 |  | 287,500 |

**11   D**

|  | Share capital Number | Share capital £ | Share premium £ |
|---|---|---|---|
| 1 Jul 20X4 | 1,000,000 | 500,000 | 400,000 |
| 1 Jan 20X5 – 1 for 4 bonus issue |  |  |  |
| (250,000 × 50p) | 250,000 | 125,000 | (125,000) |
| 1 Apr 20X5 – 1 for 10 rights issue | 125,000 | 62,500 | 125,000 |
|  | 1,375,000 | 687,500 | 400,000 |

**12   D**   200,000/5 = 40,000 shares.

Balance on share premium account becomes £75,000 + (40,000 × £1) = £115,000

**13   B**   You do not have to complete the share premium account to answer this question but it is good practice in this type of question to complete both.

### SHARE CAPITAL

|  | Number | £ |  | Number | £ |
|---|---|---|---|---|---|
|  |  |  | Bal b/d | 300,000 | 75,000 |
|  |  |  | 1 for 5 rights | 60,000 | 15,000 |
|  |  |  |  | 360,000 |  |
| Bal c/d | 480,000 | 120,000 | 1 for 3 bonus | 120,000 | 30,000 |
|  | 480,000 | 120,000 |  | 480,000 | 120,000 |

### SHARE PREMIUM

|  | £ |  | £ |
|---|---|---|---|
| 1 for 3 bonus | 30,000 | Bal b/d | 200,000 |
| Bal c/d | 227,000 | 1 for 5 rights 60,000 x 95p | 57,000 |
|  | 257,000 |  | 257,000 |

**14   D**   This error will not cause a trial balance imbalance.

**15   A**

### SUSPENSE ACCOUNT

|  | £ |  | £ |
|---|---|---|---|
| Share capital | 3,000 | Opening balance | 3,460 |
| Motor vehicles | 9,000 | Plant asset (2,800 × 2) | 5,600 |
|  |  | Closing balance | 2,940 |
|  | 12,000 |  | 12,000 |

**16   C**   (A) is wrong because labour and construction costs of building a factory would be debited to non-current assets cost. (B) is wrong because directors' remuneration would be debited to the expense account, (D) is wrong because a misposting of discount received would be a debit to suspense and a credit to the discount received account.

**17 D**

| | | £ |
|---|---|---|
| July – September | 1,000,000 × 8% × 3/12 | 20,000 |
| October – March | 750,000 × 8% × 6/12 | 30,000 |
| April – June | 750,000 × 8% × 3/12 | 15,000 |
| | 500,000 × 7% × 3/12 | 8,750 |
| | | 73,750 |

**18 C**

TAX EXPENSE

| | £ | | £ |
|---|---|---|---|
| B/d | 3,200 | Income statement (bal fig) | 27,700 |
| C/d Tax liability | 24,500 | | |
| | 27,700 | | 27,700 |

**19 B**

TAX EXPENSE

| | £ | | £ |
|---|---|---|---|
| Cash | 12,700 | B/d | 14,300 |
| C/d Tax liability | 15,600 | Income statement (bal fig) | 14,000 |
| | 28,300 | | 28,300 |

**20 C** (2) and (3)

**21 B** Statement (2) is correct. Statement (1) is incorrect because land is not usually depreciated.

**22 C** This is calculated using a T account:

DISTRIBUTION COSTS

| | £ | | £ |
|---|---|---|---|
| Cash | 130,647 | Accrual reversed | 586 |
| Closing accrual | 654 | Income statement (bal fig) | 130,715 |
| | 131,301 | | 131,301 |

**23 C** When a company makes a bonus issue it receives no monies from shareholders. Instead it issues shares to existing shareholders at par value, crediting share capital and debiting share premium account (if there is insufficient share premium then retained earnings may be debited).

Pigeon plc has 600,000 ordinary shares in issue prior to the bonus issue, because each share has a 50p par value. It therefore issues 200,000 (1/3 x 600,000) shares to shareholders, again with a par value of 50p each. The journal to record this issue is

DR   Share premium (200,000 × 50p)   £100,000
CR   Share capital                                                £100,000

The share premium account is therefore reduced to £650,000.

SAMPLE PAPER

**24 B**

TRADE AND OTHER PAYABLES

| | | | |
|---|---|---|---|
| Bank | 1,249,506 | b/d | 524,925 |
| Contra | 8,236 | | |
| Discounts received | 12,824 | | |
| | | PDB | 1,987,345 |
| c/d (bal fig) | 1,241,704 | | |
| | 2,512,270 | | 2,512,270 |

**25  B**

### TAX PAYABLE ACCOUNT

| | | | |
|---|---:|---|---:|
| Cash: Tax paid | 40,000 | b/d (bal fig) | 18,580 |
| | | HMRC refund | 2,680 |
| c/d | 23,820 | Income statement | 42,560 |
| | 63,820 | | 63,820 |

**26  B**    This is calculated using a T account:

### TAX

| | £ | | £ |
|---|---:|---|---:|
| Cash | 1,762 | Brought down | 2,091 |
| Carried down | 2,584 | Income statement (bal fig) | 2,255 |
| | 4,346 | | 4,346 |

SAMPLE PAPER

**27  D**    This is calculated using a T account:

### FINANCE COSTS

| | £ | | £ |
|---|---:|---|---:|
| Cash | 2,733 | Accrual reversed | 362 |
| Closing accrual | 419 | Income statement (bal fig) | 2,790 |
| | 3,152 | | 3,152 |

SAMPLE PAPER

**28  B**    We can assume unless told otherwise that share premium is used to the maximum possible extent when a bonus issue is made.

1 November rights issue: DR Cash £450,000, CR Share capital £50,000 (400,000 shares × 50p × ¼), CR Share premium £400,000

31 August bonus issue: CR Share capital £500,000 (500,000 shares × 50p × 2), DR Share premium £420,000 (taking the balance down to zero), DR Retained earnings £80,000

### SHARE CAPITAL

| | Number | £ | | Number | £ |
|---|---:|---:|---|---:|---:|
| c/d | 1,500,000 | 750,000 | b/d (£200,000/£0.50) | 400,000 | 200,000 |
| | | | Rights issue (400,000/4) | 100,000 | 50,000 |
| | | | | 500,000 | 250,000 |
| | | | Bonus issue (500,000 x 2) | 1,000,000 | 500,000 |
| | 1,500,000 | 750,000 | | 1,500,000 | 750,000 |

### SHARE PREMIUM

| | £ | | £ |
|---|---:|---|---:|
| Bonus issue | 420,000 | b/d | 20,000 |
| c/d | 0 | Rights (100,000 x £4) | 400,000 |
| | 420,000 | | 420,000 |

### RETAINED EARNINGS

| | £ | | £ |
|---|---:|---|---:|
| Balance of bonus (500,000 – 420,000) | 80,000 | b/d | 793,442 |
| c/d (bal fig) | 813,442 | Profit for year | 100,000 |
| | 893,442 | | 893,442 |

The two most common mistakes with this kind of question are to take the number of shares as the share capital balance as in A and D (ie to treat all shares as £1 shares), and to fail to use the share premium account to the maximum for the debit entry for the bonus issue, as in C.

**29  D**  The initial entry was one sided, so a suspense account with a credit balance of £1.9 million must have arisen in the ETB. To eliminate the suspense account a debit entry of £1.9 million is required. The rights issue is 1 for 4, so (3,000,000/4) = 750,000 × 20p shares are issued, giving a credit of £150,000 in the share capital account. The share premium is therefore (3.60 – 0.20) = £3.40 per share, which gives a credit to the share premium account of 750,000 × £3.40 = £2,550,000. The remainder of the journal is to record the amount unpaid on the shares ((750,000 × £3.60) – £1,900,000) = £800,000 as an other receivable:

| | | |
|---|---|---|
| DR  Suspense | £1,900,000 | |
| DR  Other receivables | £800,000 | |
| CR  Share capital | | £150,000 |
| CR  Share premium | | £2,550,000 |

**30  A**  The purchases day book and cash book figures are transactions occurring during the year, so when we open the T account with these figures we know there has been no opening journal reversing the accruals and prepayments as at the end of the previous year. Instead of being told opening and closing accruals and prepayments you are told the difference between them. You need to think carefully therefore about the side of the T account on which the net difference should appear. Where there is a decrease in the accrual the net effect is a credit in the expense account, while a decrease in a prepayment will be a net debit in the expense account.

PURCHASES

| | £ | | £ | |
|---|---|---|---|---|
| PDB | 9,801 | Decrease in accruals | 75 | |
| CB | 107 | Income statement (bal fig) | 9,893 | (A) |
| Decrease in prepayments | 60 | | | |
| | 9,968 | | 9,968 | |

Note that in option B the net differences are the wrong way round; option C ignores the cash book amount, while option D ignores the effect of accruals and prepayments entirely.

**31  A, B**  If a company is no longer a going concern then the directors have concluded that it will not trade for the foreseeable future (ie less than twelve months) and so all non-current assets and liabilities are transferred to current assets and current liabilities respectively (A).

All assets are valued at their resale or break-up value, which is the expected selling price in a forced sale position (B). This is likely to be a substantially lower value than carrying amount for assets such as fixtures and fittings acquired recently. An exception to this may arise in the case of properties, of which Wombat plc has none.

Although not being a going concern means the directors believe the company is likely to cease trading within 12 months, it does not necessarily mean that it will cease trading immediately (C), nor that a liquidator will be appointed immediately (D).

**32  C**  When a bonus issue is made you should assume that the share premium account is used as far as possible, with only the remainder being debited to retained earnings.

SHARE CAPITAL

| | £ | | £ |
|---|---|---|---|
| c/d | 500,000 | b/d | 300,000 |
| | | Bonus issue (300,000/3 × 2) | 200,000 |
| | 500,000 | | 500,000 |

SHARE PREMIUM

| | £ | | £ |
|---|---|---|---|
| Bonus issue | 150,000 | b/d (300,000 × £0.50) | 150,000 |
| | 150,000 | | 150,000 |

## RETAINED EARNINGS

| | £ | | £ |
|---|---|---|---|
| Bonus issue (200,000 – 150,000) | 50,000 | b/d | 717,000 |
| c/d | 667,000 | | |
| | 717,000 | | 717,000 |

33  C, D Delivery vehicle costs, including depreciation, are part of distribution costs (C) because they are part of the cost of providing customers with the final product. These costs are completely independent of the original purchase cost of the product Albion plc manufactures.

Carriage inwards is part of the overall cost of bringing materials to their current condition and location. As such they should be included in inventory costs, and thus cost of sales (D).

34  C

### TAXATION ACCOUNT

| | £ | | £ |
|---|---|---|---|
| Tax paid | 123,090 | b/d | 114,520 |
| c/d (bal fig) | 137,100 | Income statement | 145,670 |
| | 260,190 | | 260,190 |

35  C  The total interest charge for the year should be:

New debentures (£120,000 × 6% × 3/12) = £1,800

Original debentures (£400,000 × 6%) = £24,000 (= cash paid)

Therefore the closing accrual should be £1,800, giving a total trade and other payables total of (246,800 + 1,800) = £248,600

### TRADE AND OTHER PAYABLES

| | £ | | £ |
|---|---|---|---|
| c/d | 248,600 | b/d | 246,800 |
| | | Accrual | 1,800 |
| | 248,600 | | 248,600 |

### INTEREST

| | £ | | £ |
|---|---|---|---|
| Cash | 24,000 | b/d | 0 |
| Accrual (trade and other payables) | 1,800 | Income statement | 25,800 |
| | | (400,000 x 0.06) + | |
| | | (120,000 x 0.06 x 3/12) | |
| | 25,800 | | 25,800 |

**36 C**

CASH BOOK

| | £ | | £ |
|---|---|---|---|
| | | b/d | 2,643 |
| | | Paying in slip (1) | 90 |
| | | Dishonoured cheque (2) | 1,988 |
| c/d (bal fig) | 4,721 | | |
| | 4,721 | | 4,721 |

*Bank reconciliation statement*

| | £ |
|---|---|
| Balance per bank statement | (9,647) |
| Lodgement uncleared (5,016 – 90) | 4,926 |
| Balance per cash book | (4,721) |

The cash balance of £160 should not be offset against the overdraft as there is no right of offset.

**37 D**

SHARE PREMIUM ACCOUNT

| | £ | | £ |
|---|---|---|---|
| Bonus issue (400,000/4 x 0.10) | 10,000 | b/d | 840,000 |
| | | (400,000 x (2.20 – 0.10)) | |
| | | Preference shares | 22,500 |
| | | (45,000 x (1.00 – 0.50)) | |
| Bal c/d | 852,500 | | |
| | 862,500 | | 862,500 |

**38 C**

BONUS ACCOUNT

| | £ | | £ |
|---|---|---|---|
| Bank | 34,682 | b/d | 9,653 |
| | | Income statement (bal fig) | 37,791 |
| c/d | 12,762 | | |
| | 47,444 | | 47,444 |

| 1 | D | Generally accepted accounting practice |
|---|---|---|

2   B   By law it is the board of directors which is responsible for preparing financial statements.

3   B   False. Creditors falling due after more than one year are non-current liabilities.

    C   True.

4   D   There are only (25 – 10 + 10 – 10) = 15 units in stock at the end of January. 10 of these are valued at £55, and the remainder at £54:

        (10 × £55) + (5 × £54) = £820

5   C   Cash raised is 250,000 × £3.55 = £887,500, which is debited to cash at bank. The credit to share capital is 250,000 × £2 = £500,000, while the credit to share premium is 250,000 × £1.55 = £387,500

SAMPLE PAPER

6   A

| | £ |
|---|---|
| Retained profits at 1.1.X8 | 4,695,600 |
| Operating profit | 520,000 |
| Debenture interest (£1.3m x 10%) | (130,000) |
| Tax | (156,000) |
| Retained profits at 31.12.X8 | 4,929,600 |

SAMPLE PAPER

7   A   The bonus issue of shares (A) would be recorded in the financial statements using the journal: DR Share premium, CR Share capital.

        Options B, C and D would initially be recorded in the cash book.

8   C

| | £ |
|---|---|
| Share capital | 50,000 |
| Share premium (£50,000/£0.25 x £(0.40 – 0.25)) | 30,000 |
| Retained profits reserve | 107,594 |
| General reserve (bal fig) | 20,000 (C) |
| Closing net assets | 207,594 |

**1    D**

|  | £ | £<br>A | £<br>B | £<br>C |
|---|---|---|---|---|
| Profit | 520,000 | | | |
| | 40,000 | | | |
| | 560,000 | 280,000 | | |
| | | (40,000) | | |
| | | 240,000 → 160,000 | 80,000 | |
| | | | | |
| | | 280,000 → 140,000 | 84,000 | 56,000 |
| | 520,000 | 300,000 | 164,000 | 56,000 |

**2    D**

| Share | 3:<br>Lisa<br>£ | 3:<br>Mary<br>£ | 4<br>Olga<br>£ | Total<br>£ |
|---|---|---|---|---|
| Salary | 35,000 | | 20,000 | 55,000 |
| Interest on capital | 25,000 | 20,000 | 15,000 | 60,000 |
| Interest on drawings | (7,000) | (3,500) | (4,000) | (14,500) |
| Residual profit (3:3:4) | 374,850 | 374,850 | 499,800 | 1,249,500 |
| | 427,850 | 391,350 | 530,800 | 1,350,000 |

**3    C**

### MARY'S CURRENT ACCOUNT

| | £ | | £ |
|---|---|---|---|
| Drawings | 35,000 | Bal b/d | 150,000 |
| Bal c/d | 506,350 | Profit share | 391,350 |
| | 541,350 | | 541,350 |

**4    D**

| Shares<br>Shares | 3:<br>5:<br>Declan<br>£ | 2<br>3:<br>Indiah<br>£ | 2<br>Calum<br>£ | Total<br>£ |
|---|---|---|---|---|
| 1 Jan to 30 June: 450,000/2 | 135,000 | 90,000 | | 225,000 |
| 1 July to 31 Dec: | | | | |
| Salaries (6 months) | | 20,000 | 24,000 | 44,000 |
| Profit (£225,000 – 44,000) | 90,500 | 54,300 | 36,200 | 181,000 |
| | 225,500 | 164,300 | 60,200 | 450,000 |

**5    B**    Profit For appropriation: £32,000 – £250 = £31,750

| Shares | 1:<br>Billy<br>£ | 1<br>Charlie<br>£ |
|---|---|---|
| Opening balance | 15,500 | 12,700 |
| Loan interest | 250 | |
| Interest on capital (5% x £20,000; £30,000) | 1,000 | 1,500 |
| Profit share | 14,625 | 14,625 |
| Closing balance | 31,375 | 28,825 |

**6　A**

| Share<br>Share | 3:<br>10:<br>Curtis<br>£ | 2<br>5:<br>Sillett<br>£ | 5<br>McAllister<br>£ | Total<br>£ |
|---|---|---|---|---|
| To 31 December 20X5 (£480,000 × 6/12) | 144,000 | 96,000 | | 240,000 |
| To 30 June 20X6 (£480,000 × 6/12) | | | | |
| Salaries 6/12 | | 10,000 | 6,000 | 16,000 |
| PSR | 112,000 | 56,000 | 56,000 | 224,000 |
| | 256,000 | 162,000 | 62,000 | 480,000 |

**7　A**　The petrol bills have been debited to motor vehicle expenses. This is incorrect and should be reversed (so credit motor vehicle expenses). Because they are private expenses of the partner they should be debited to his drawings account.

**8　C**　Added to profit in allocating the profit among the partners

**9　B**　Interest on partners' capital is an appropriation of profit (debit appropriation account). Since partners have earned the money by their investment in the business, their current accounts should be credited with it. (Option D would be theoretically possible, but most firms maintain current accounts separately from capital accounts in order to record such items.)

**10　B**

| Shares<br>Shares | 2:<br>5:<br>P<br>£ | 1<br>3:<br>Q<br>£ | 2<br>R<br>£ | Total<br>£ |
|---|---|---|---|---|
| Profit share January to June (120,000) | 80,000 | 40,000 | | 120,000 |
| Profit share July to December (120,000) | 60,000 | 36,000 | 24,000 | 120,000 |
| | 140,000 | 76,000 | 24,000 | 240,000 |
| Guarantee amount | (1,000) | | 1,000 | |
| | 139,000 | 76,000 | 25,000 | 240,000 |

**11　D**　Interest payable by partners increases the amounts of profits available for appropriation (credit appropriation account). It must be charged against the partners' current accounts (debit partners' current accounts).

**12　A**　Note the question asks for Charity's residual profit share, not her total profit share.

| Shares | 3:<br>Faith<br>£ | 2:<br>Hope<br>£ | 1<br>Charity<br>£ | Total<br>£ |
|---|---|---|---|---|
| Interest on capital | 1,600 | 1,200 | 960 | 3,760 |
| Salary | | 8,000 | | 8,000 |
| Residual profit shares(3:2:1) | 36,120 | 24,080 | 12,040 | 72,240 |
| | 37,720 | 33,280 | 13,000 | 84,000 |

**13　B**

| Shares | 1:<br>P<br>£'000 | 1<br>Q<br>£'000 |
|---|---|---|
| January to June (340 − ((340 + 20)/2)) | 160 | |
| July to December (180/2) | 90 | 90 |
| | 250 | 90 |

**14 B** Profit in first 6 months is ((400,000 + 40,000)/2) - £40,000) = £180,000

| | | 3: | 1: | 1 | |
|---|---|---|---|---|---|
| Shares | | 5: | 3: | 2 | |
| Shares | | G | H | I | Total |
| | | £ | £ | £ | £ |
| To 30 June | | | | | |
| Salaries (6 months) | | | 20,000 | 10,000 | 30,000 |
| Profit | | 90,000 | 30,000 | 30,000 | 150,000 |
| To 31 Dec (400 + 40)/2 | | 110,000 | 66,000 | 44,000 | 220,000 |
| | | 200,000 | 116,000 | 84,000 | 400,000 |

**15 B**

Profit for July to Dec (540,000 + 30,000)/2 – 30,000 = £255,000
Profit for Jan to June (570,000/2) = £285,000

| | £ |
|---|---|
| X profit share July to Dec £255,000 x 2/3 | 170,000 |
| X profit share Jan to June £285,000 x 50% | 142,500 |
| | 312,500 |

**16 A**

| | | 3: | 1: | 1 | |
|---|---|---|---|---|---|
| Shares | | 3: | 2: | 1 | |
| Shares | | G | H | I | Total |
| | | £ | £ | £ | £ |
| July to December – salaries (6 months) | | | 10,000 | 10,000 | 20,000 |
| Profit share (380/2 – 20) | | 102,000 | 34,000 | 34,000 | 170,000 |
| January to June – salary (6 months) | | | | 10,000 | 10,000 |
| Profit share (380/2 – 10) | | 90,000 | 60,000 | 30,000 | 180,000 |
| | | 192,000 | 104,000 | 84,000 | 380,000 |

**17 C** The corrected account looks like this.

CURRENT ACCOUNT

| | £ | | £ |
|---|---|---|---|
| Drawings | 6,200 | Balance b/d | 270 |
| Balance c/d | 7,070 | Interest on capital | 2,800 |
| | | Salary | 1,500 |
| | | Net profit | 8,700 |
| | 13,270 | | 13,270 |

**18 B** When the error is corrected there will be a credit entry of £8,000 to rent receivable.

A would be an additional debit entry making the difference larger, C would be an equal debit and credit and D is simply moving the debit from one account to another.

**19 A** £340 credit

SUSPENSE ACCOUNT

| | £ | | £ |
|---|---|---|---|
| Opening balance | 500 | Allowance for receivables | 840 |
| Closing balance | 340 | | |
| | 840 | | 840 |

Error 1 requires a debit to the receivables account and a credit to sales with no effect on suspense. Error 2 is simply moving the credit from one account to another with no effect on suspense.

**20 C** A is a debit to the wrong account and B is correct. D is double entry although the wrong way round.

**21 C** The accrual should have increased expenses by £400 but instead expenses were decreased by £400 leading to an overstatement of profit of £800.

**22 A** £4,000 tax + £5,900 rent = £9,900

|  | £ |
|---|---:|
| *Rent* | |
| 1 June 20X7 to 31 December 20X7 = 7/12 × £5,400 | 3,150 |
| 1 January 20X8 to 31 May 20X8 = 5/12 × £6,600 | 2,750 |
| | 5,900 |
| *Local property tax* | |
| 1 June 20X7 to 31 March 20X8 = 10/12 × £3,900 | 3,250 |
| 1 April 20X8 to 31 May 20X8 = 2/12 × £4,500 | 750 |
| | 4,000 |

**23 C**

|  | £ |
|---|---:|
| 3,080 × 9/12 | 2,310 |
| 3,080 ×100/110 × 3/12 | 700 |
| | 3,010 |

**24 A** Understated by 2 × £475 = £950

**25 B**

|  | £ |
|---|---:|
| Decrease in net assets | 11,025 |
| Capital introduced | 14,000 |
| Drawings (875 × 12) | (10,500) |
| Drawings | (2,625) |
| Loss | 11,900 |

**26 A** Use the accounting equation:

|  | £ |
|---|---:|
| Net assets at 31.12.X8 | 32,500 |

|  | £ |
|---|---:|
| *Owner's interest* | |
| Opening capital | 23,000 |
| (= opening net assets) | |
| Capital introduced | 4,000 |
| Profit (balancing figure) | 8,750 |
| Drawings (2,500 + 750) | (3,250) |
| | 32,500 |

Goods drawn by owner are taken at cost

**27 C**

|  | £ |
|---|---:|
| Increase in net assets | 127,000 |
| Add drawings | 47,000 |
| Deduct capital paid in | (25,000) |
| Net profit | 149,000 |

**28 A**

|  | £ |
|---|---:|
| Opening net assets | 266,800 |
| Capital introduced | 50,000 |
| Drawings | (40,000) |
| Profit (balancing figure) | 9,600 |
| Closing net assets | 286,400 |

29  B,D  Owner's capital (A) and drawings (C) relate to capital; income tax payable (E) does not feature in a sole trader's balance sheet.

30  C

31  B  Errol is credited with £50,000 x 3/8 = £18,750, then debited with £50,000 x 3/4 = £37,500, a net debit of £18,750

32  A  The correcting journals in full are:

|  |  | £ | £ |
|---|---|---|---|
| DR | Debtors | 180 |  |
| CR | Cash |  | 180 |
| | | | |
| DR | Sales (2 x 12) | 24 |  |
| CR | Debtors |  | 24 |

So the net correcting journal (A) is

|  |  | £ | £ |
|---|---|---|---|
| DR | Debtors | 156 |  |
| DR | Sales | 24 |  |
| CR | Cash |  | 180 |

33  A, C, E

Share premium (B) and dividends paid (D) are found only in company financial statements. Fixed assets (A) is a UK GAAP term which can be seen in the financial statements of sole traders, partnerships or some limited companies. Partners take drawings (C) rather than dividends. Profit for the year (E) can be found in any financial statements

34  B  Using the balance sheet equation:

|  | £ |
|---|---|
| Closing net assets (1,726 + 2,387) (B) | 4,113 |
| Drawings | 15,000 |
| Opening net assets | (5,000) |
| Net profit (B) | 14,113 |

35  C  Errol is a partner for the whole year, receiving 3/8 of the first 8 months profit, and 3/4 of the last 4 months after Sayhan's retirement:

|  | £ |
|---|---|
| £121,248 x 8/12 x 3/8 = | 30,312 |
| £121,248 x 4/12 x 3/4 = | 30,312 |
|  | 60,624 |

36  A, D  In the absence of a drawings account on the ETB the debit for drawings should be to capital, since it reduces the amount of the owner's interest in the business (A). To remove the incorrect entry from other expenses the account needs to be credited (D).

37  A,D  On the ETB net profit is a debit to the profit and loss account (A) and a credit to the balance sheet (D).

38  B  John is credited with £50,000 x 3/10 = £15,000, then debited with £50,000 x 5/8 = £31,250, a net debit of £16,250

| Share | 1 | 1 | 1 | | 3 | 2 | 1 |
|---|---|---|---|---|---|---|---|
| | Ines | Alex | Sebastian | | Ines | Alex | Sebastian |
| | £ | £ | £ | | £ | £ | £ |
| Drawings | 7,500 | 7,500 | 7,500 | b/d | 10,490 | 12,020 | 20,170 |
| Goodwill (60,000@ 1:1) | 30,000 | | 30,000 | Profit (87,750@ 3:2:1) | 43,875 | 29,250 | 14,625 |
| c/d | 46,865 | | 7,295 | Goodwill (60,000@ 3:2:1) | 30,000 | 20,000 | 10,000 |
| Loan a/c | | 53,770 | | | | | |
| | 84,365 | 61,270 | 44,795 | | 84,365 | 61,270 | 44,795 |

Note that you would have arrived at Answer B if you had ignored Sebastian's £7,500 drawings.

**40   C**

| | £ |
|---|---|
| Net profit before interest | 122,000 |
| Interest (50,000 x 8% x 6/12) | (2,000) |
| | 120,000 |
| Partner salaries (20,000 + 25,000) | (45,000) |
| Residual profit for appropriation (5/8 and 3/8 x 75,000 = 46,875 and 28,125) | 75,000 |

| Share | 5 | 3 | |
|---|---|---|---|
| | Shula | Kenton | |
| | £ | £ | |
| Salaries | 20,000 | 25,000 | |
| Residual profits | 46,875 | 28,125 | |
| Total | 66,875   (B) | 53,125   (C) | |

Note that in option A the interest is not deducted from net profit before it is appropriated, while in option D a full year's interest is deducted.

**41   D**   Burgess has overpaid Lever in error by sending two cheques, and this overpayment will need in future to be refunded. The important thing at this stage is to make sure that the accounting entries are correct.

The first cheque should not have been sent as it was for the full amount, even though settlement discount of £52 was available. It was recorded correctly by Burgess however:

DR   Lever      £2,606

CR   Cash      £2,606

Only the second cheque should have been sent to Lever, for £2,554 (2,606 – 52). This second cheque was recorded only as:

CR   Cash      £2,554

so a debit balance arose on a suspense account of £2,554. In addition, no entry was made for the discount received.

The correcting journal must therefore clear the suspense account and credit discounts received, the debit entry being to record the amount due for refund from Lever:

DR         Lever                £2,606

CR         Suspense             £2,554

CR         Discounts received  £52

42   A,E   Goods taken by a partner count as drawings in the same way as does cash (A), and no salaries are appropriated to partners unless they specifically agree that they should be (E).

Interest on drawings by a partner (B) are negative appropriations of profit, not income. Interest on a partner's loan capital (C) is an expense in the profit and loss account, not income. Drawings by a partner are debited to the current account, not credited (D).

43   C   Interest on drawings is an appropriation of profit. It affects neither the partnership's net profit available for appropriation nor the cash position. Drawings, rather than interest on them, affect the cash position.

44   C   In the absence of a formal agreement the Partnership Act 1890 states that partners shall receive no interest on their fixed capital contributions, but that they shall receive interest at 5% per annum on loans to the partnership. Josh's loan has been outstanding for three months in the financial year so he is entitled to: £40,000 x 5% x 3/12 = £500 (C).

45   B

|  | £ |
|---|---|
| Opening net assets | 40,000 |
| Net profit | 117,000 |
| Capital injection | 30,000 |
| Drawings (£3,200 x 12) | (38,400) |
| Stock drawings (£7,200 x 100/160) | (4,500) |
| Closing net assets | 144,100 |

46   A

|  | £ |
|---|---|
| Opening capital (39,400 + 15,600 + 11,500 – 10,200 + 6,600) | 62,900 |
| Capital introduced | 3,000 |
| Profit for year (bal fig) | 15,800 |
| Drawings ((12 x 750) + 500) | (9,500) |
| Closing capital (46,000 +18,900 + 8,400 – 7,500 + 6,400) | 72,200 |

47   D   Loss on sale of fixed assets should be added back to net operating profits.

48   D

|  | £ |
|---|---|
| Add: depreciation charge | 980,000 |
| Less: profit on sale of assets | (40,000) |
| Less: increase in stocks | (130,000) |
| Add: decrease in debtors | 100,000 |
| Add: increase in creditors | 80,000 |
| Addition to operating profit | 990,000 |

49   B   Depreciation should be added back as it not a cash flow. Proceeds from sale of fixed assets appear under the heading 'Capital expenditure and financial investment' and are not included as an adjustment to profit in order to reach net cash flow from operating activities.

50   C   1   The direct and indirect methods will give the same figure

      2   A rights issue of shares is a cash flow

      4   The profit on sale of a fixed asset appears as an adjustment to profit in order to reach net cash flow from operating activities

51   D   The depreciation charge and the increase in creditors should both have been added.

# REVIEW FORM – ACCOUNTING QUESTION BANK

Your ratings, comments and suggestions would be appreciated on the following areas of this Question Bank:

|  | Very useful | Useful | Not useful |
|---|:---:|:---:|:---:|
| *Number of questions/answers* | ☐ | ☐ | ☐ |
| *Standard of answers* | ☐ | ☐ | ☐ |

|  | Excellent | Good | Adequate | Poor |
|---|:---:|:---:|:---:|:---:|
| *Overall opinion of this Question Bank* | ☐ | ☐ | ☐ | ☐ |

**Please add further comments below:**

**Please return to:**

The Learning Team
Learning and Professional Department
**ICAEW**
Metropolitan House
321 Avebury Boulevard
Milton Keynes
MK9 2FZ
ACAFeedback@icaew.com
www.icaew.com